Asian Americans in Class

Asian Americans in Class

CHARTING THE ACHIEVEMENT GAP AMONG KOREAN AMERICAN YOUTH

Jamie Lew

FOREWORD BY JEAN ANYON

Teachers College, Columbia University
New York and London

To Maya

Published by Teachers College Press, 1234 Amsterdam Avenue, New York, NY 10027

Library of Congress Cataloging-in-Publication Data

Lew, Jamie.
Asian Americans in class : charting the achievement gap among Korean American youth / Jamie Lew; foreword by Jean Anyon.
p. cm.
ISBN 0-8077-4694-0 (cloth alk. paper) — ISBN 0-8077-4693-2 (pbk. : alk. paper)
1. Korean Americans—Education—United States. 2. Children of Immigrants—Education—United States. 3. Academic Achievement—United States. I. Title.

LC3501.K6L49 2006
371.82995'7073—dc22 2005046747

ISBN-13:
978-0-8077-4693-6 (paper)
978-0-8077-4694-3 (cloth)

ISBN-10:
0-8077-4693-2 (paper)
0-8077-4694-0 (cloth)

Printed on acid-free paper
Manufactured in the United States of America

13 12 11 10 09 08 07 06 8 7 6 5 4 3 2 1

Contents

Foreword

Stereotypically, Asian Americans are the model minority group, a standard by which other minorities are measured, and typically found wanting. Many people assume that Asian American students are uniquely prepared for rigorous academics by a homogeneous Asian culture and are therefore uniformly educationally triumphant, supported throughout by parents who have worked their way from immigrant poverty to economic comfort.

Jamie Lew's book powerfully interrupts these traditional beliefs. She points out, for example, that many Asian American families in the United States are poor: They are almost twice as likely as White families to live in poverty; almost one in four Asian American families earned less than $25,000 in 2000. In New York City, where Lew's research is based, approximately 24% of Asian American children lived in poverty in 2003.

The research at the heart of this myth-challenging book is a qualitative study of Korean high school students and their peer networks, families, and schools. Lew's study reveals that significant support in these areas is crucial to student success. She found that Asian American students' academic achievement is not just a matter of cultural attitudes and hard work, although these may be important. Rather, educational achievement has crucial determinants in what money and social capital can buy.

The middle-class students Lew studied were afforded private tutoring by their parents, attended well-resourced schools, and had access to Korean American peers who could supply information about applying to college. The working-class students, on the other hand, lived in families forced by lack of jobs and income to move from place to place; the children attended poorly resourced schools; and they had friendship networks whose participants did not have information about higher education. Lew reports that a good many of these working-class students became alienated from school and ultimately dropped out. Most entered the minimum-wage workforce.

This story of differential access by social class parallels the tale research tells about other U.S. youth. As I discovered years ago, the resources available to White students differed dramatically according to the social class context in which the schools I studied were embedded. While more affluent Whites attended schools with myriad materials and opportunities to excel, schools attended by working-class Whites offered a rote, pencil and paper curriculum with little creativity, rigor, or meaning to the students (Anyon, 1980, 1981). We also know that low-income (working-class) Black and

Latino youth most often attend schools that do not have the resources to support high achievement (see Anyon, 1997, and Natriello & Pallas, 1990, among others). And the peer networks to which low-income Black and Latino youth have access typically do not provide support for college-going or educational achievement (Stanton-Salazar, 2001).

Lew also highlights the salience of race and uncovers discrimination against the students. She examines how race intersects with class, and the ways in which this process affects academic achievement among Asian American students. The outcome of her research I accentuate here is the corroboration she provides of the power of social class and race to play a determining role in educational outcomes. Like other poor minority children and youth, Asian American students typically need the finances and social support that middle-class status provides in order to succeed educationally. This finding is powerful evidence that we must look beyond the classroom for ways to improve the education and life chances of poor students.

We must look, I believe, at the public policies that make monetary and social support possible for some education systems and families, and nearly impossible for others. I have argued at length that public policies (like those that keep the minimum wage at poverty levels and keep public transit from connecting urban areas and job-rich suburbs), inequitable tax laws, and racial discrimination in hiring and housing maintain both familial and institutional poverty in U.S. cities and low-income suburbs, where most poor students live (Anyon, 2005). These and other public policies deprive low-income schools and families—especially those who are not White—of the finances and social resources they need to support sustained educational achievement.

Jamie Lew's book is an important resource, not only in the effort to overturn an unfortunate stereotype but in the effort to demonstrate that children of the working poor cannot be expected to excel without the nurturing that buttresses the achievement of the more affluent.

—Jean Anyon
The Graduate Center, CUNY

REFERENCES

Anyon, J. (1980). Social class and the hidden curriculum of work. *Journal of Education, 162*, 67–92.

Anyon, J. (1981). Social class and school knowledge. *Curriculum Inquiry, 11*, 3–42.

Anyon, J. (1997). *Ghetto schooling: A political economy of urban educational reform*. New York: Teachers College Press.

Anyon, J. (2005). *Radical possibilities: Public policy, urban education, and a new social movement*. New York: Routledge.

Natriello, G., & Pallas, A. (1990). *Schooling disadvantaged children: Racing against catastrophe*. New York: Teachers College Press.

Stanton-Salazar, R. (2001). *Manufacturing hope and despair: The school and kin support networks of U.S.-Mexican youth*. New York: Teachers College Press.

Acknowledgments

Throughout the years of writing this book, I have benefited from more people than I can possibly acknowledge. I would like to begin by thanking the Institute on Ethnicity, Culture, and the Modern Experience and the Joseph C. Cornwall Center for Metropolitan Studies at Rutgers University–Newark for helping fund this research. I owe special thanks to Clem Price and Charles Russell, whose leadership at the Institute has provided invaluable guidance to me and other junior faculty at Rutgers. I am grateful to all of my colleagues at Rutgers, with special thanks to Alan Sadovnik who has been a mentor and constant source of encouragement and support. I am also deeply indebted to my students at Rutgers, who continue to challenge and inspire me.

I have benefited greatly from friends and colleagues who have read parts of this book in various forms and given me support: They include Jean Anyon, Sherri-Ann Butterfield, Lin Goodwin, Phil Kasinitz, Rosamond King, Stacey J. Lee, Vivian Louie, Pedro Noguera, Kimberly A. Scott, and Ricardo Stanton-Salazar. As a graduate student, I was fortunate enough to receive counsel from advisors who made my research at the Magnet High School possible. Special thanks to Gita Steiner-Khamsi, Celia Genishi, Gary Natriello, and Gary Okihiro, who provided invaluable insight and friendship throughout my years at Teachers College, Columbia University. I would also like to thank Dr. Nash and Becky Baek for their belief in the project and for supporting the research during my years at Magnet High.

Having worked in the Asian American community in New York City for many years, I am deeply moved and inspired by the work of the many human service and advocacy organizations as well as the community leaders, parents, and children who strive for equal opportunities in their daily lives. I am especially grateful to Won Kang and Songyun Kang, who provided insight and guidance during my research with the high school dropouts. I am indebted to Won for his keen observation of and commitment to the youths and their family. I am genuinely grateful to Songyun for being an advocate of this project and for encouraging me to write a book about Korean American youths in order to give voice to those who have yet to be heard. To that end, I will forever be indebted to the high school students who trusted me and shared their experiences, stories, and lives with me. Without them, this book would not have been possible.

During the last months of writing this book, I was fortunate enough to be invited to the Asian Pacific American Institute at NYU as a visiting scholar. I am deeply grateful to John Kuo Wei Tchen and all of the staff at APA for including me in their community of scholars, and for allowing me to finish my book. I am continually inspired by their work in and commitment to Asian American studies and communities.

I wholeheartedly thank my editor, Brian Ellerbeck, and his team at Teachers College Press, whose intelligence, patience, and commitment to this book have been invaluable. Special thanks to Adee Braun for her insightful and timely support.

It is impossible to even imagine writing this book without my parents, whose strength and vision have provided the foundation for my dreams. They have taught me and my brother to believe in ourselves and to be true to our hearts. This book is a product of their teaching and counsel. My brother, Johnny Lew, has never ceased to amaze me with his patience, kindness, and intelligence. I am grateful for his endless support and friendship.

Finally, I owe my deepest gratitude to my husband and best friend, Larry Lerner, who has given me the courage to conceive, write, and finish this book. As my personal editor, he has presided over all stages of this book: research, writing, editing. Throughout the years, he spent countless hours helping me with the manuscript and encouraged me to continue when I wanted to give up. In the last months of completing the final manuscript, we have been graced with another beginning—the birth of our daughter, Maya, and it is to her I dedicate this book. As I look into her eyes, I have never been so clear as to why I needed to write this book.

CHAPTER 1

Matters of Class, Race, Ethnicity, and Schools: A Structural Analysis of Asian American Achievement

POST-1965 ASIAN AMERICANS: CHANGING DEMOGRAPHICS

Since the mid- to late 1960s, a significant number of U.S. immigrants have come from countries in Africa, Asia, Central and Latin America, and the West Indies. In 2000, the foreign-stock population (the foreign-born and their U.S.-born and -raised children) reached nearly 55.9 million, or one-fifth of the total U.S. population (U.S. Bureau of the Census, 2001). Unlike the earlier waves of immigrants at the turn of the 20th century, post-1960s immigrants have come mostly from non-European countries; more than 50% of all U.S. immigrants in recent decades have been from Latin America and more than 25% from Asia (Suárez-Orozco, 2001).

Nowhere is this shift in U.S. immigration reflected more starkly than in the changing demographics of children of immigrants. Children of immigrants are indeed the fastest-growing segment of the U.S. child population; one out of every five children age 18 and under are the children of an immigrant (Urban Institute, 2000). Immigrants and their children are predominantly settling in urban areas, with California and New York taking the lead. It is estimated that half of California's children have an immigrant parent, while 31% of New York's children fall into this same category (Ruiz-de-Valasco & Fix, 2000; Urban Institute, 2000).

This rapid growth in the number of the children of immigrants over the last few decades has raised important questions about their adaptation to and impact on American society. Among the many U.S. institutions grappling with this issue, public urban schools, in particular, have undergone dramatic transformation. While some children of immigrants are achieving in school and acquiring economic mobility, others are performing below their native-born peers and reproducing the plight of the poor minority underclass. The structural and cultural factors that determine such trajectories among children of immigrants are critical and timely issues facing our schools and the nation (Portes & Rumbaut, 1996, 2001; Ruiz-de-Valasco & Fix, 2000; Suárez-Orozco, 2001; Suárez-Orozco & Suárez-Orozco, 2001).

Among children of immigrants, Asian Americans represent one of the fastest-growing student populations in U.S. schools. It is estimated that approximately 2.6 million Asian American children are enrolled in the nation's nursery, kindergarten, elementary, and high schools, accounting for 5% of the total student enrollment (U.S. Bureau of the Census, 1999). This is a marked increase from 1972, when Asian American school-age children accounted for a mere 1%. Much of this increase is attributed to recent immigration patterns; 88% of all school-age Asian American children have a foreign-born parent, compared with 65% of Hispanic children and 20% of all U.S. children. Moreover, a significant percentage of Asian American children live in urban areas and attend city public schools: according to the 2000 census, a remarkable 96% of Asian immigrants live in metropolitan areas, with 45% of them residing in central cities; in New York City, approximately 90% of all school-age Asian American children are enrolled in public elementary and high schools (Asian American Federation of New York, 2001).

Accompanying this influx of Asian American children has been notable attention paid to their academic achievement and educational success. Asian American children, in the aggregate, are more likely than Whites, Blacks, or Hispanics to have higher GPAs, math SAT scores, and college-graduation rates (Hsia, 1988; Kao & Tienda, 1998; Sue & Okazaki, 1990). Touted as "whiz kids" and labeled as a "model minority," Asian American children have captured headlines in the mainstream media, represented as the American Dream fulfilled.

The significant number of academically achieving Asian American students notwithstanding, these aggregate data fail to distinguish important variability within and among Asian American communities—differences such as ethnicity, language, class, generation, and immigration history to name a few (S. Lee, 2004; S. J. Lee, 1996; Lew, 2004, in press; Louie, 2004). Moreover, the aggregate data do not reveal the increasing number of Asian American children who are failing and dropping out of school (Lew, 2003a, 2004). For instance, among 513,000 Asian American high school students in the nation, an estimated 25,000 dropped out of high school. This represents a dropout rate of 4.8% for Asian Americans, the highest rate since 1995 (U.S. Bureau of the Census, 1999). That is, studies show that along with the increasing rate of high-achieving Asian American students, there is also a growing high school dropout, reflecting a widening achievement gap within the Asian American student population.

Take the case of New York City public schools: while Asian Americans account for approximately 13% of the city's high school students, they make up a disproportionately large percentage of students in the city's most elite magnet high schools—48% at Stuyvesant, 46% at Bronx Science, and 39%

at Brooklyn Tech (Division of Assessment and Accountability, 2000, 2002). However, the dropout rate for Asian American high school students in New York City between 1997 and 2002 has steadily risen from 8% in 1997 to 9% in 1998, 10% in 1999, 11.1% in 2000, and 12.2% in 2002.

These statistics reveal an important trajectory of Asian American students' school achievement and social mobility. However, since the data on Asian American academic achievement is rarely broken down to account for class difference, researchers often overlook this all-important structural factor and how it affects school performance. When we carefully examine the increasing class bifurcation within Asian American communities, however, the widening achievement gap is less surprising.

While many Asian American families have seen economic success, many others are poor. In 1998, 1.4 million Asian Americans (about 13%) and 15.8 million non-Hispanic Whites (about 8%) were poor. About 18% of Asian Americans under the age of 18 were poor, compared to 11% of non-Hispanic White children (U.S. Bureau of the Census, 1999). Although approximately 33% of Asian American families reported an annual income of $75,000 or more (versus 20% for non-Hispanic White families), 21% made less than $25,000 a year (versus 19% for non-Hispanic Whites). Furthermore, Asian American families were almost twice as likely as non-Hispanic White families to live in poverty (11% versus 6%). Among the Asian American families in poverty, 8% were two-parent households, while 29% were headed by single women (non-Hispanic White families were at 4% and 21%, respectively) (U.S. Bureau of the Census, 1999).

The poverty rate of Asian American children, particularly those in urban areas such as New York City, is equally daunting. It is estimated that nearly one in four Asian American children in New York City live in poverty—that is, roughly 24% came from households falling below $17,063 in annual income for a family of four. This surpasses the poverty level of non-Hispanic White children in the city (16%), that of all U.S. children (17%), and that of Asian American children nationwide (14%) (Asian American Federation of New York, 2003; U.S. Bureau of the Census, 1999).

Despite the changing demographics, achievement gap, and class variance among them, Asian Americans are nevertheless seen as a homogeneous group, a model minority that is uniformly excelling in school and achieving economic mobility. Explanations for this status have historically focused on a cultural argument emphasizing "Asian" values of education, the work ethic, and nuclear families (De Vos, 1973, 1980; Mordkowitz & Ginsberg, 1987; Sung, 1987). While this cultural dimension is undoubtedly significant, the model minority and cultural arguments miss crucial aspects of Asian American students' experiences. First, homogenizing Asian Americans essentializes them, implying they have a fixed "ethnic" experience that accounts for their success. Second, the model minority discourse ignores important historical and social contexts for framing Asian American experience. Third, the portrayal of Asian Americans as model minorities has historically been used as a wedge between minorities by implying that if Asians can make it, then all minority groups should be able to achieve academically, as long as they uphold the values of education, hard work, and a nuclear family that Asians supposedly prize. This focus on individualism and meritocracy inherent in the model minority discourse buoys the culture-of-poverty argument that runs in tandem with it. As such, model minority discourse ignores critical structural factors such as class, race, gender, and schooling resources that serve to contextualize Asian American students' academic performance, while ignoring those children who are living in poverty, failing or dropping out of high school, and facing downward mobility (Fong & Shinagawa, 2000; Hune & Chan, 2000; Hurh & Kim, 1984; Kiang & Kaplan, 1994; Lee, 1996; Lew, 2003a, 2004, in press; Louie, 2004; Pang & Cheng, 1998; Park, Lee, & Goodwin, 2003; Weinberg, 1997).

In order to address the limitations of the cultural argument, researchers have focused on important structural factors such as immigration history, economic context, and opportunity structure to explain Asian American achievement. For instance, it has been argued that selective migration of post-1965 immigrants—namely, those entering under professional status—favored those who are coming with a higher education level and from higher socioeconomic backgrounds. That is, Asian American children's educational success can be largely attributed to those who are coming from Asian families who were middle-class professionals in their country of origin (Barringer, Gardner, & Levin, 1993; Hirschman & Wong, 1986). Researchers have also underscored ethnic economies and networks as important means for Asian Americans to achieve social mobility. Although ethnic economies have been historically formed as a result of racial and social barriers, as well as lack of access to the primary-sector-market economy, researchers argue that this avenue allows Asian immigrants to gain important economic and social resources for first- and second-generation immigrants (Hirschman & Wong, 1986; Light & Bonacich, 1988; Portes & Rumbaut, 1996, 2001). While highlighting the structural and economic conditions into which the immigrant groups become situated, Portes and colleagues note the significance of strong co-ethnic networks and ethnic economies, which help promote social mobility for immigrants and their children. Particularly for those residing in poor and isolated urban communities, strong social capital in the form of entrepreneurship, local churches, and co-ethnic networks provides important economic and social resources for first-generation immigrants and their second-generation children. It is argued, therefore, that post-1965 Asian immigrants and their children are able to achieve in school and gain economic opportunities as a result of their ethnic economy and ties to immigrant networks (Portes & Rumbaut, 1996, 2001; Portes & Zhou, 1993; Rumbaut & Cornelius, 1995; Zhou & Bankston, 1996, 1998).

The significance of these studies notwithstanding, there are still glaring gaps in research on Asian American children and education. For instance, although earlier studies emphasize immigration history and economic contexts to situate the contemporary Asian American experience, there is still little understanding of how variability of class *among* Asian American communities may impact their educational outcome. For instance, how does class variability *within* the ethnic economy impact second-generation outcome, particularly for those children attending high schools in urban context? How do Asian immigrant parents, from varying socioeconomic backgrounds, adopt different educational strategies for their children?

In addition, there is limited understanding of those Asian American students who are failing or dropping out of high school and thus facing downward mobility. How do class variability and network orientation impact academic achievement among Asian American students? For those who are failing or dropping out of high school, how do these structural factors, for instance, impact their academic aspirations and achievement differently from those students who are achieving in schools? Moreover, there are inadequate explanations of the racial incorporation of Asian Americans in general, and of how they may negotiate their racial and ethnic identities in different social and economic contexts.

One of the more glaring gaps is how school context and educational resources impact the academic achievement of Asian American students. How does school as an institution limit and advance their educational opportunities? In different schooling contexts, how do Asian American students from varying socioeconomic backgrounds learn to cross cultural and linguistic borders between immigrant homes and mainstream schools as a way to access important institutional and educational resources? As active agents, how do Asian American children themselves learn to adapt to or resist their ties to immigrant parents' ethnic networks, while negotiating relationships with key agents in mainstream institutions such as school? Overall, there is dearth of research that critically examines how structural factors of class, race, and school context may impact academic aspirations and achievement of Asian American students. This book is an attempt to address some of these important and timely questions.

In order to explore these questions in depth, this research is based on a case study of one of the fastest-growing post-1965 Asian ethnic groups —Korean Americans. Drawing from interviews over a 3-year period with 72 Korean American youths in New York City urban schools, this research compares and contrasts the experiences of two groups of second-generation Korean American students: (1) 42 students attending an elite magnet high school and (2) 30 high school dropouts attending a community-based GED program (General Educational Development test for a high school equivalency diploma). By comparing these two groups of Korean American students, the research shows how Korean students' academic achievement and aspirations are fundamentally based on critical structural factors of class, race, and schooling resources.

CO-ETHNIC NETWORKS, SOCIAL CAPITAL, AND CLASS

This research supports earlier studies that emphasize the significance of co-ethnic networks and social capital among Asian American families (Gans, 1992; Hirschman et al., 1999; Kasinitz et al., 2004; Light & Bonacich, 1988; Portes & Rumbaut, 1996, 2001; Rumbaut & Cornelius, 1995; Zhou & Bankston, 1996, 1998). The findings illustrate how the academically achieving Korean students at a magnet high school, compared to Korean high school dropouts, are more likely to gain important educational information and resources from their co-ethnic network. However, the findings also show the importance of the variability of class and network orientation within the co-ethnic communities and who benefits more from such enclaves (Kasinitz, Mollenkopf, & Waters, 2004; Kwong, 1996; Lee, 2004; Lew, 2004, in press; Sanders & Nee, 1987). Although Korean Americans have been homogeneously touted for their entrepreneurial success and middle-class status, this study points to the socioeconomic variability within co-ethnic networks and examines how the difference in social-class backgrounds and network orientation impact educational strategies employed by the two groups. For instance, this study shows that while most of the parents of the academically achieving students at the magnet high school are middle-class entrepreneurs, most of the parents of the high school dropouts are working-class employees of co-ethnic entrepreneurs and do not own their own businesses. A greater percentage of Korean high school dropouts, compared to the magnet high school students, come from single-parent households, which further limits their family income. Moreover, the dropouts were more likely to live in and attend schools in isolated poor neighborhoods.

The class distinction and neighborhood incorporation become particularly significant when examining the ways in which members of co-ethnic networks access and accumulate social capital. For instance, how educational information and potential resources from co-ethnic networks actually become accessed and utilized by the members integrally depends on members' socioeconomic backgrounds, status position within the networks, and access to institutional resources both in *and* outside co-ethnic networks. In other words, one can not effectively analyze the schooling aspirations and achievement of second-generation Korean and other Asian American youths without taking into account key structural and institutional factors, such as their parents' socioeconomic backgrounds and educational level, the advantages *and* limitations of ethnic networks, and the students' access to institutional resources in schools.

While accounting for the benefits of co-ethnic networks for immigrant communities, it is also important to note that the process of gaining access to and accumulating social capital is far from neutral, but instead is stratified by class, race, and gender (Bourdieu, 1977; Lareau, 1987, 2003; Lin, 1990, 2000; Noguera, 2003; Saegert, Thompson, & Warren, 2001; Stanton-Salazar, 1997, 2001). If social capital is conceived as resources embedded in social networks used for purposive action, then different networks will accumulate and provide different sets of resources in accordance with the social and economic status of individuals within those networks. That is, human capital and social capital are integrally related: the education level, occupational status, and socioeconomic backgrounds of the individuals bear directly on the strength of the network. It follows, then, that middle-class White parents have a far greater advantage in gaining access to social capital than do poor minority parents, especially minority single mothers (Lareau, 1987; Saegert et al., 2001; Stanton-Salazar, 1997, 2001). The structures in place for the former allow their children to access gatekeepers who can provide important school and professional resources. On the other hand, poor minority students living and attending schools in isolated low-income communities are at a particular disadvantage in gaining access to these important institutional gatekeepers. In fact, the latter are often literally cut off from capital, networks, and institutional resources that are needed for gaining jobs, college admission, and opportunities for moving into the mainstream economy (Anyon, 1997; Massey & Denton, 1993; Noguera, 2003; Orfield & Eaton, 1996).

SCHOOL CONTEXT: SIGNIFICANCE OF INSTITUTIONAL RESOURCES

Numerous studies have shown that gaining social capital in school—that is, forming relations with guidance counselors, teachers, and other community gatekeepers who are integrally connected to institutional resources—is pivotal for academic achievement and social mobility (Croninger & Lee, 2001; Fine, 1991; Natriello, McDill, & Pallas, 1990; Stanton-Salazar, 2001). In his research on kinship and network ties among Mexican American youths in California, Stanton-Salazar (2001) argues that social capital is valuable insofar as members in a network have access to institutional agents—those aforementioned gatekeepers who are able to provide minority and immigrant children with access to resources and opportunities in mainstream institutions.

This study supports Stanton-Salazar's findings, noting the significance of institutional agents for Korean American students, including teachers, counselors, clergy, community leaders, college-going youth in the community, school peers, as well as members in the children's kinship networks who can provide information about school programs, college admission, and career decision making.

The findings also illustrate that although immigrant parents may be able to provide strong co-ethnic networks that are extremely important for their children, they are rarely in a position to act as institutional agents themselves because of their limited English skills and knowledge of the U.S. education system. How the Korean parents in different social and economic contexts negotiate and resist these limitations is part of the more subtle and significant findings in this research. For instance, in order to mitigate their limitations regarding the English language and knowledge of the U.S. education system, the Korean parents of students at magnet high school were more likely to hire private tutors and counselors who could act as institutional agents for their children. The magnet high school parents readily enrolled their children in private, tuition-based, after-school academies as a way to provide them with additional schooling and college counseling. These academies, called *hagwon*, mostly located in Korean ethnic enclaves, provide tutorials on school subjects and standardized exams, as well as bilingual college counselors. It is through these agents, who are often bilingual and have schooling experiences in U.S. colleges and work experiences in the mainstream economy, that many of the immigrant parents at the magnet high schools were able to provide a means for their children to receive concrete schooling and career information, accommodate for limited bilingual resources available at the school, and provide an important institutional and linguistic bridge between themselves and their American-born and -raised children. In contrast, the low-income Korean high school dropouts rarely attended hagwon, since their parents could not afford the tuition. Instead, most of them had to work after school to compensate for their limited family income. Consequently, their parents predominantly relied on their children's public schools for educational and counseling support; however, the Korean high school dropouts in this study attended urban schools with limited educational and bilingual resources for effectively assisting them in school. Furthermore, the dropout students, as a result of economic, neighborhood, and school factors, readily changed residence and high schools throughout their young adulthood. This high mobility and school transfer rate decreased the likelihood of accumulating social capital while increasing the chances of alienation from and dropping out of high school.

This book reminds educators how children of immigrants, particularly those who are poor and racial minorities, need to learn how to move outside the parameter of their immigrant parents and families in order to access resources and opportunities in mainstream institutions such as schools (Phelan,

Davidson, & Yu, 1993; Stanton-Salazar & Dornbusch, 1995). However, this process of crossing institutional borders between home and school proves difficult for many minority and immigrant children (Bourdieu & Passeron, 1977; Boykin, 1986; Gee, 1989; Neisser, 1986). Phelan and her associates (1993) describe several different kinds of barriers to crossing such institutional borders: sociocultural, socioeconomic, linguistic, and structural barriers. They note that these barriers, based on power relations, carry the potential to induce in minority students experiences of anxiety, depression, and fear that inhibit them from performing school tasks. They argue that these barriers further hinder their social development, including their ability to establish supportive relationships with teachers, peers, and other institutional agents who can help them navigate through schooling and cross institutional boundaries.

It is important to note that while much attention has been placed on the benefits of co-ethnic networks of first-generation parents and their role in providing educational resources for their children, there has been little understanding of what role, if any, the second-generation Asian children play in accessing institutional agents and accumulating social capital for themselves, particularly in school context (Lew, 2003b). Who are the institutional agents found in school and ethnic communities, and how do these agents help the students cross institutional and linguistic borders between home and schools? How do second-generation children as active agents adapt to and resist their parental immigrant networks? How do the students construct their own peer networks in communities and schools to compensate for the limitations of their immigrant parents, while accumulating institutional resources that they specifically need in schools?

As this research demonstrates, neither the high- nor low-achieving Korean American students regularly turned to their first-generation immigrant parents for schooling or college guidance, given the latter's limited English language skills and knowledge of the U.S. education system. Ultimately, both groups of second-generation Korean American students built peer networks at school to compensate for their immigrant parents' limitations, but the resources embedded in each of their networks differed greatly. The magnet high students drew on their networks to build a pool of institutional resources who could help them with schooling, the college application process, and future career opportunities in the mainstream economy. Meanwhile, the high school dropouts had limited access to gatekeepers in and outside of their poor-quality inner-city schools. Rather, they were far more likely to navigate through schooling alone and isolated, using their networks instead to access low-wage jobs within the ethnic enclave or to pursue other nonacademic options, such as enlisting in the army.

Moreover, the students' widely disparate schooling contexts provided them with equally disparate educational resources. For instance, the Korean

American students at the magnet high school attended an academic high school revolving around a college-preparatory program populated predominantly by middle-class White and Asian students with access to institutional agents such as teachers and counselors who could provide important educational resources. On the other hand, the Korean high school dropouts attended neighborhood urban schools with high poverty and dropout rates populated predominantly by working-class poor minorities and recent immigrant students with limited access to institutional agents in school. That is, most of the high school dropouts were concentrated in high-poverty urban schools troubled by a shortage of teachers, counselors, and instructional resources capable of accommodating the growing number of minority and limited–English proficient (LEP) students. In such different schooling contexts, the two groups of Korean American students adopted different educational and racial strategies to adapt to, negotiate, and resist their given opportunity structure.

By highlighting the actual processes and practices available to students, this study identifies the important institutional characteristics and key actors critical to building social capital. And by looking at how second-generation youths from varied socioeconomic backgrounds and schooling contexts access and accumulate social capital, this research highlights the significance of peer networks and gatekeepers, who can provide access to mainstream institutional resources advancing academic achievement.

The findings reveal how middle-class parents and their children at the magnet high school, compared to working-class parents of high school dropouts, are more likely to *overcome* schooling and language limitations while *advancing* educational opportunities. This book illustrates how Asian families' class position and network orientation may affect the nature and quality of their children's education, and how the cumulative effects of social, economic, and cultural resources to overcome limited schooling resources are deeply implicated in the reproduction of social inequalities.

BECOMING AMERICAN: SALIENCE OF CLASS, RACE, AND ETHNICITY

If schools and class matter for Asian American children, so does race. After all, for minorities who emigrate to the United States, it is impossible to separate becoming "American" from the historical construction of Whiteness and the invisible norm associated with being "White." Because Africans, Asians, Latin Americans, and Native Americans have been historically placed in opposition to the ideal of "Whiteness" and have signified what "Whiteness" is not, some argue that the long historical exclusion of racial minorities and racialized ethnic groups from Whiteness must be critically examined in order to better understand the experiences of today's immigrants (Kibria, 2002; Okihiro, 1994; Omi & Winant, 1986).

The salience of race and ethnicity is well illustrated in studies of "symbolic" ethnicity and how roles of ethnicity take on different meanings for Whites and racial minorities. Studies show that White European ethnic groups are privileged in adopting a "symbolic ethnicity"—ethnic identification that is voluntary and subjective in character, with individuals able to claim aspects of their ethnic heritage and ancestry at their own discretion (Alba, 1990; Gans, 1979; Waters, 1990). In her research on White European ethnic groups (third generation and later), Waters (1990) found that her subjects exercised the option to symbolically express their ethnic affiliations how and when it best suited them, depending on the context.

However, racial minorities do not always enjoy this option. For instance, Black Americans are tagged with a racial label that obfuscates their ethnic identities, whether their older or more recent ancestries stem from parts of Africa, Central and South America, or the West Indies. Therefore, by being labeled "Black," they do not readily exercise an option to express their ethnicity (Butterfield, 2004; Foner, 1985; Waters, 1994, 1999).

Asian Americans are also subject to racial categorization that is ascriptive rather than voluntary—a process that is based on power relations of self and "other" (Espiritu, 1994; Tuan, 1998). As Espiritu (1994) explains, racial categorization is a "process whereby a more powerful group seeks to dominate another, and in so doing, imposes upon these people racial categorical identity that is defined by reference to their inherent difference from or inferiority to the dominant group" (p. 251). For instance, in her study of middle-class Asian Americans (of the third and later generations), Tuan (1998) found that her subjects were seen as perpetually foreigners and non-Americans, with Whiteness being the invisible norm for being identified as "American."

Ogbu's (1987) research on race and school achievement points out the importance of students' cultural frame of reference and their interpretation of economic, social, and political barriers. He notes that for some African American students, a low school performance is a form of adaptation to their limited social and economic opportunity in adult life. Ogbu argues that as a way to develop survival strategies to endure barriers such as inferior schooling, job ceilings, and racial discrimination, involuntary immigrants, such as African Americans, learned to form an oppositional cultural frame of reference and oppositional social identity to dominant white society. The survival strategies become a collective struggle, referred to as a fictive kinship, encouraging behaviors that are not conducive to school and academic success (see, e.g., Fordham & Ogbu, 1986; Gibson & Ogbu, 1991; Matute-Bianchi, 1986; Ogbu, 1987; Suárez-Orozco & Suárez-Orozco, 1995, 2001). Historically, a number of studies have found that minority groups define their identity vis-à-vis the dominant groups, with minority identity being based on an oppositional cultural frame of reference (Castle & Kushner, 1981; De Vos, 1980; Ogbu, 1987; Spicer & Thompson, 1972).

Expanding on Ogbu's theory, studies on post-1965 immigrants have been complicating the dichotomy of voluntary and involuntary groups. For instance, studies show that children of Black immigrants who are living in poor, isolated communities, without the protections of strong co-ethnic networks, are also likely to adopt an oppositional cultural frame of reference that may not be conducive to schooling success. However, what is glaringly absent from this literature is how Asian American children who are poor, low-achieving, and dropping out of high school may be negotiating their racial and ethnic identities, and how this process may be similar to and different from other racial groups' experiences. Moreover, we have less understanding, in general, of how the process of racial and ethnic identity construction may change according to different social and economic contexts.

For instance, some crucial questions remain unanswered: How do Asian American children from varied socioeconomic backgrounds and schooling contexts negotiate their race and ethnic identities, and to what extent does this process affect their academic achievement? More specifically, in the context of a Black-and-White racial discourse, how are working-class Asian American students who attend poor-quality urban schools populated mostly by poor minorities negotiating their racial and ethnic identities, and how does this process compare to those of middle-class Asian American students attending elite urban schools populated mostly by middle-class Whites and Asians? Looked at from another angle, how do Asian Americans, as a racial minority, negotiate being labeled a model minority on the one hand (which aligns them with Whiteness and "American" values) and forever foreign and non-American on the other?

By drawing an integral relationship between class and race, this research illustrates the complex processes by which students negotiate multiple and hybrid identities. Despite the fluidity of race and ethnic identities among Korean American students, however, both groups of students nevertheless face racism, often labeled foreigners and marginalized as non-Americans. However, given their different economic, community, and schooling contexts, the two groups of Korean American students adapt to racial marginalization differently.

Embedded in strong and supportive networks at home and in school, Korean students at the magnet high school were better protected from the stratifying forces of racism and poverty. In addition, they learned to use education as a strategy to withstand racial discrimination, firmly believing that because of their status as a racial minority, they had to work even harder in school to gain opportunities. The Korean high school dropouts, on the other hand, disassociated from Whiteness and aligned their experiences with those of their mostly low-income, racial minority peers—Asians, Blacks, and Hispanics. Moreover, the high school dropouts distinguished themselves from the "wealthy" and "studious" Koreans and other Asians, whose attributes of "success" they associated with Whiteness. As a form of resistance and adaptation to the limited opportunities both in and outside of their communities, the dropouts adopted an oppositional cultural frame of reference and rejected schools as an effective means of achieving economic mobility. This study pays particular attention to the varied ways in which the two groups of Korean American youths interpret their different opportunity structures and systemic racism, and how these structural factors intersect with their cultural outlook on schooling aspirations and achievement.

ASIAN AMERICANS AS A MODEL MINORITY: REVISITING THE STEREOTYPE

Asian American students are far from a homogeneous group: They actively adapt, negotiate, and resist changing structural forces to create and re-create their cultures. Although both groups of Korean American students and their parents believed that education was important and wanted their children to do well, their ability to translate such aspirations into concrete school achievement varied widely and depended on important structural factors. In short, race, class, and schools *do* matter for Asian American children. This book examines *how* they matter—as they pertain to academic aspirations and achievement among Asian American children in an urban context.

We would do well to remember how the model minority discourse has historically been used as a wedge between minorities, particularly in light of the federal mandate of the No Child Left Behind Act and high-stakes testing, both of which emphasize test scores and mere outcomes. During the 1960s, many on the left looked askance at what was the precursor to this cultural explanation for Asian achievement. In vogue at the time was the "culture-of-poverty" argument used to explain the failures of certain U.S. minorities, especially African Americans. By attributing the social problems and poverty of American Blacks to their "unstable family structure" and "culture of poverty," researchers and policy makers blamed the Black community alone for its place in society (Glazer & Moynihan, 1963)—ignoring structural factors and stressing individualism and meritocracy. Not surprisingly, the left responded by asserting that this culture-of-poverty argument oversimplified a more complex predicament and was tantamount to blaming the victims for their socioeconomic woes. In time, however, this argument was nonetheless flipped and applied to Asian American achievement. As Woo (2000) explains that culture of poverty ideas would "resurface in a new form, namely, through an inverted discourse that premised achievement on an enabling cultural repertoire of values associated with Asian Americans as 'model minorities'" (p. 194). So, as the argument was used to chastise Blacks and elevate Asian Americans, the wedge was put in place to play minorities off against one another, reproducing and sustaining the ideology of individualism and meritocracy while ignoring fundamental structural issues. As Woo (2000) points out, "Where issues of social inequality in matters of race and ethnicity are concerned, Asian Americans occupy a critical place in our thinking about ethnic politics. They are not only a common empirical reference point for evaluating relative progress and achievement among different groups but an ideological one as well" (p. 194).

But the image of Asian Americans as a model minority persists, not least because it is upheld by many as an entirely positive representation. Unfortunately, it also conceals disparities among Asian American children and deemphasizes the important structural barriers faced by poor and minority children. In the end, the model minority discourse attributes academic success *and* failure to individual merit and cultural orientation, while neglecting the important institutional resources that all children need in order to achieve academically. What is needed is a more nuanced analysis taking into account the changing and complex relationship between cultural and structural factors, which can better explain varied schooling experiences among Asian American children. In this book, I examine some of the key cultural and structural factors that help contextualize Asian American educational experiences—pre- and post-immigration patterns, race and ethnic relations, socioeconomic backgrounds, and schooling contexts—using Korean Americans in New York City as a case study to elaborate further.

POST-1965 KOREAN AMERICANS: NATIONWIDE AND IN NEW YORK CITY

Over the last few decades, Asian Americans have been one of the fastest-growing populations in the United States. During the 1940s, some 250,000 Asian Americans lived in the United States, a mere 1% of the population (Hing, 1993). By 1990, that number had risen to 7.3 million, with more than 13 different ethnic populations falling into the Asian category (U.S. Bureau of the Census, 1993). According to the 2000 census, the Asian population had increased to 11.9 million, or 4.2% of the total U.S. population (U.S. Bureau of the Census, 2001).

The Immigration Reform Act of 1965 ushered in a new era for Asians seeking admission into the United States, and with its occupational preference system and family reunification provisions, it initially favored and attracted a significant number of middle-class professionals from Asia—many of whom are the parents of the academically achieving Asian American children in U.S. schools today. Since then, Asian American communities have become more diverse in terms of class and occupational status. Yet we know very little of Asian American children who are coming from working-class immigrant parents.

In the case of Korean American communities, their changing demographics could be explained, in part, by the changing migration pattern. According to Kim (1981), initially the majority of the post-1965 Korean Americans were college-educated, urban, middle-class professionals in Korea. And by and large, they were young; more than 90% who entered between 1966 and 1975 were under the age of thirty-nine (p. 25). In addition, a disproportionate number (nearly half) were Christians (Kwon, Kim, & Warner, 2001).

However, Korean American communities are also becoming more diversified in class, education level, and professional status. According to Light and Bonacich (1988), between 1966 and 1977, a significant number of Korean immigrants entered the United States under the professional status and family reunification quota. But as more relatives emigrated to the States and became citizens, Koreans took further advantage of family reunification and kinship preferences: This latter category accounted for 66% of all Korean immigrants in 1967; by 1981, it had increased to 92% (Light & Bonacich, 1988). As the number of Korean immigrants coming under family reunification increased, the education level of Korean immigrants decreased: According to Hurh and Kim (1984), between 1965 and 1969, 44% of Korean Americans had completed four or more years of college; that number shrank to 31.7% between 1970 and 1974, and to 25.7% between 1975 and 1980 (see also Lee, 2004).

Furthermore, as more Korean immigrants arrived under family reunification and kinship-based chain migration, many settled in certain cities because their family and kin already resided there (Kim, 1981; Light & Bonacich, 1988; Min, 1995, 1996; Portes & Rumbaut, 1996, 2001). Moreover, Korean Americans exhibit less ethnic and linguistic diversity than other Asian ethnic groups; unlike the Chinese and South Asians, for instance, whose populations come from various countries and regions and speak multiple languages and dialects, Korean Americans consist predominantly of one ethnic group, mostly from South Korea, speaking one language (Min, 1995, 1996). Such shared language, ethnicity, and immigration history among the post-1965 Korean Americans help explain how Korean American communities have been able to form strong ethnic enclaves and network ties throughout the United States.

By 2000, Korean Americans were one of the largest and fastest-growing populations among post-1965 Asian ethnic groups (U.S. Bureau of the Census, 2002). In 1990, there were approximately 800,000 Koreans in the United States; by 2000, the Korean population had increased to approximately 1.2 million. In addition, among those in the 1990 statistic, more than 600,000 were foreign-born—meaning that because of the recent influx, a majority of Korean Americans today are either first or second generation (Chan, 1991; Takaki, 1989). Moreover, by the mid-1990s, a majority of foreign-born Korean Americans lived in urban areas, with Los Angeles and New York City containing the two largest Korean Americans populations (National Association of Korean American Service and Education Consortium, 1998).

In New York City, an overwhelming 80% Korean Americans are foreign-born and Korean Americans are the third-largest Asian ethnic group, at approximately 91,000, with over 70% concentrated in Queens, followed by 14% in Manhattan. In light of this, it is no surprise that nearly 40% of the Korean Americans in New York City are labeled as LEP (speaking English "not well" or "not at all"). This percentage indicates greater language barriers faced by Koreans than by adult New Yorkers overall, of whom only 13% are labeled as LEP (Asian American Federation of New York, 2002).

In addition, Korean Americans in New York City have a median household income of $37,094, below both the Asian American average of $41,119 and overall city average of $38,293. That said, Korean Americans in New York City were less likely to be in poverty than the total city population: Approximately 17% (15,002) of Koreans in New York City lived below the poverty line, compared with 21% overall. Meanwhile, 14% (2,532) of Korean children lived in poverty, compared with 24% of all Asian American children and 30% of the city's children overall (Asian American Federation of New York, 2002).

RESEARCH SITES AND METHODS

As mentioned earlier, this study is based on in-depth interviews with a total of 72 Korean American youths attending urban high schools in New York City: 42 Korean students attended one of the elite magnet high schools, which I call Magnet High, or MH; 30 Korean high school dropouts attended a GED preparatory program at a nonprofit organization, which I call Youth Community Center, or YCC. My informants included both second-generation children born and raised in the United States, with at least one Korean-born parent, and 1.5-generation children born in Korea but raised in the United States since at least age 10, with at least one Korean-born parent. For the purpose of this research, I define both groups as second-generation. The students' ages ranged from 14 to 20. All names of schools, organizations, and students are pseudonyms.

In addition to the interviews, the study also draws on a background survey, document analysis, and observation. The survey was used to gather information about students' backgrounds: place of birth (and, if born in Korea, their length of residence in the United States), place of residence, age, gender, names of high schools attended, grade level completed, bilingual skill, affiliation with the Korean ethnic community, parents' level of education and occupation, and eligibility for the reduced-cost or free lunch programs (see accompanying table).

Students' Background

	Share of Respondents (%)		
	Magnet High	*GED*	*Total*
Male	36	60	48
Female	64	40	52
1.5 generation	38	40	39
2nd generation	62	60	61
Single-parent household	12	40	26
Eligible for free or reduced-price lunch	36	80	58
Mother graduated from college	60	30	45
Father graduated from college	64	30	47
Lives in Queens	79	90	85
Has at least one parent working in ethnic economy	60	80	70
Has at least one parent who owns his or her own business	53	13	33
Has at least one parent working for a co-ethnic entrepreneur	7	67	37
	(N = 42)	(N = 30)	(N = 72)

An overwhelming 85% of the Korean American students interviewed lived in Queens, the borough with the largest Korean American population: broken down further, 79% of the students at MH resided in Queens, as did 90% of the high school dropouts at YCC. Although the majority of students lived in Queens, the two groups came from different backgrounds. The MH students came from higher socioeconomic backgrounds and a greater number of two-parent households. For instance, 36% of the students at MH were eligible for reduced-cost or free lunch, compared to 80% of the high school dropouts at YCC. Moreover, 12% of MH students came from single-parent households (usually headed by mothers, and restricted to a single source of income), compared to 40% of the high school dropouts at YCC. An additional 10% of the dropouts lived with distant relatives and/or friends.

Education level was high among MH parents; approximately 60% of the mothers and 64% of the fathers had graduated from college. In addition, 20% of the mothers and 22% of the fathers held graduate degrees. Among the dropout parents, approximately 30% of the mothers and 30% of the fathers had graduated from college. None of the dropout parents had graduate degrees.

Occupationally, an overwhelming 70% of the parents in both groups worked in the ethnic economy: the breakdown was 60% of the MH parents and 80% of the dropout parents. However, class disparity between the two groups of parents become more evident when assessing their occupational status *within* the ethnic economy. Viewed from a different angle, although 60% of the students at MH had at least one parent working in the ethnic economy, 53% of them owned their own businesses, while only 7% worked for co-ethnic entrepreneurs. On the other hand, 80% of the high school dropouts had at least one parent working in the ethnic economy; only 13% of them ran their own business, while 67% worked for co-ethnic entrepreneurs. Furthermore, the occupational status of those parents who did not work in the ethnic economy also varied: While a majority of the parents at MH worked in professional occupations, such as law, medicine, or education, the majority of the parents at YCC worked in sales, the service economy, and civil service jobs.

It is important to point out that class variance existed *within* each group: Some of the Korean American students at MH came from working-class families, while some of the high school dropouts at YCC came from middle-class families. However, in the aggregate, the two groups of Korean American students clearly represented different socioeconomic backgrounds and were divided along class lines. Given the students' eligibility for the free or reduced-price lunch program, as well as the parents' level of education and occupational status, I refer to the Korean American students at MH as coming mostly from middle-class families and the high school dropouts at YCC as coming mostly from working-class families.

Magnet High School (MH)

As a competitive elite high school in New York City, MH prides itself on student academic achievement paralleled by few public high schools. According to the annual school report (New York City Board of Assessment, 2003), approximately 2,700 students were enrolled, and since entrance to the school is based on a competitive standardized exam, students commute to the school from all five of New York City's boroughs. Almost half of the students were Asian (46.5%), while 37% were White, 9.1% Hispanic, and 7.4% Black. Only about 1% consisted of recent immigrants to the United States (those who had immigrated within the last 3 years).

Approximately 99% of the students graduated and pursued a 4-year college education. An overwhelming 97% graduated with a Regents Diploma, 2.2% with a local diploma, and less than 1% with a GED diploma. Students' average SAT scores were 626 verbal and 671 math (scores on each segment of this test range from 200 to 800), compared to the average of 443 verbal and 472 math for New York City schools. Meanwhile, students' academic performance correlated to their socioeconomic backgrounds. From 2001 to 2003, the percentage of MH students eligible for the reduced-price or free lunch program was 19.5 (2001), 19.3 (2002), and 25.2 (2003); by comparison, schools citywide averaged 48.4 (2001), 51.3 (2002), and 54.0 (2003).

Approximately 97% of the teachers were fully licensed and permanently assigned to the school. Teachers with a master's degree or higher totaled 84.9% (2002) and 90.5 % (2003). In addition to the qualified teaching staff, the school has college guidance counselors who meet with students during their junior year in preparation for the college application process. Based on a rigorous college-preparatory curriculum, the school offers Advanced Placement (AP) courses in humanities, social science, and natural science.

Youth Community Center (YCC)

The Youth Community Center is a nonprofit community-based organization in Queens. Although the organization provides social service programs to diverse racial and ethnic communities, it primarily serves Korean Americans in Queens. Its education and outreach programs provide students and adults with counseling, tutoring, classes on the Test of English as a Foreign Language (TOEFL), English-as-a-second-language (ESL) classes, and preparatory classes for the General Educational Development (GED) exam.

All of the Korean students in the GED program had officially dropped out of their respective neighborhood public high schools in New York City and had been referred to the program by teachers, counselors, parents, community members, and peers. The Korean high school dropouts in the GED program came from various public high schools in New York City, most of which had a record of low student academic performance and high school dropout rates, as well as a disproportionate number of poor minority students and recent immigrants. Since the students came from numerous schools, it is difficult to give detailed information and statistics for all of them. However, as a point of reference, I will cite statistics from one particular urban high school in Queens, New York, since it was the one most commonly attended by the Korean American high school dropouts.

According to the annual school report (New York City Board of Assessment, 2003), the school had approximately 2,400 students, most whom lived in Queens. Almost half were Hispanic (45.4%), while 25.6% were Asian, 22.4% Black, and 6.6% White. Approximately 18%—compared with

10% of high school students citywide—were recent U.S. immigrants (those who had immigrated within the last 3 years). Among these recent immigrants, 20% were from Korea, 20% from Ecuador, and 40% from China.

Academically, the students struggled: 42.3% had graduated on time, 34.8% were still enrolled, and 22.8% had dropped out. Only 26.5% of the students graduated with a Regents Diploma, 73.5% with a local diploma, and less than 1% with a GED diploma. Students' average SAT scores were 419 verbal and 460 math (scores on each segment of this test range from 200 to 800), compared to the average of 443 verbal and 472 math for New York City schools. Meanwhile, a disproportionate number of students were eligible for the reduced-price or free lunch program, which reveals their low socioeconomic backgrounds. Between 2001 and 2003, the percentage of eligible students steadily rose from 47.7 (2001), to 60.4 (2002), to 70.3 (2003); the citywide average was 48.4 (2001), 51.3 (2002), and 54.0 (2003). Teacher qualifications were not quite on par with the magnet high school: Approximately 90% of the teachers were fully licensed and permanently assigned to the school; the percentage of teachers with a master's degree or higher was 77.2% (2002) and 78.6% (2003).

ORGANIZATION OF THE BOOK

Part I examines the educational strategies employed by Korean immigrant parents. Divided into Chapter 2 (Korean American students at the magnet high school) and Chapter 3 (Korean American high school dropouts), this part demonstrates how different social and economic contexts affect the two groups of Korean parents, leading them to adopt divergent educational strategies for their children. On the surface, the two groups of parents have much in common, including limited English skills and knowledge of the U.S. education system, as well as strong aspirations for their children to excel in school and gain opportunities that they were not afforded as immigrants. However, the two groups differed greatly in their socioeconomic backgrounds, pre- and post-immigrant status, ties to co-ethnic networks, and access to schooling resources—all key structural factors that placed the parents of the Magnet High students at a greater advantage in providing their children with economic support and schooling resources.

Part II examines educational strategies adopted by the second-generation Korean American students in the school context. Divided into Chapter 4 (Korean American students at the magnet high school) and Chapter 5 (Korean American high school dropouts), this part shows how the institutional character of the schools themselves promotes or hinders the students' access to key gatekeepers such as teachers and counselors, individuals who could provide important schooling resources that many of the students could not obtain from their immigrant parents. By placing Korean students' experiences in two different schooling contexts, these chapters illustrate the disparate institutional barriers that each group faces as well as the different racial and educational strategies they adopt in order to resist and overcome these barriers.

For many children of Asian immigrants, school and home represent two disparate realities with very different cultural codes and discourses. How the students traverse these institutional boundaries is influenced by many structural and cultural factors, including socioeconomic backgrounds, co-ethnic networks, neighborhood incorporation, school resources, and race and ethnic relations among them. The findings show that these factors intersect most poignantly in the workings of second-generation youth networks and peer relations in schools and communities. As active agents rather than mere passive recipients, both groups of students negotiate and resist their opportunity structure by constructing youth networks and using them to gain the institutional support they need in a mainstream institution such as school. However, since they come from different economic, community, and schooling contexts, they find different information and resources embedded in their respective peer networks. Ultimately, the process is far from neutral; instead, it is deeply divided along class and racial lines.

Chapter 6 outlines education policy recommendations based on the findings of this research. It underscores the significance of class, race, and school resources as they bear on academic achievement among Asian American students, at the same time challenging the Asian American stereotype as a model minority and the culture-of-poverty argument that deemphasize the structural resources that all children need. Clearly, the influx of children of post-1965 immigrants and their concentrated settlement in metropolitan areas pose a new set of challenges for our urban schools. Education policy should reflect this changing demographic in order to better serve these students, who are increasingly diverse in language, ethnicity, immigration history, and socioeconomic background.

PART I

Growing Up with Immigrant Parents: Parental Strategies and Co-Ethnic Networks

Academic achievement among Asian American children has been most commonly attributed to the beliefs, attitudes, and values of their Asian parents. While culture certainly plays a role here, this argument homogenizes Asian American families and children, ignoring crucial variation within communities and, in so doing, essentializing this population by constructing a group with fixed "Asian" experience and identities. Lost in this reductionistic portrayal is a crucial issue: Asian American parents in different social and economic contexts adopt different strategies to educate their children, and these patterns affect their children's academic achievement.

What is needed is a more nuanced analysis taking into account structural factors, the relationship between culture and structural issues, and how cultures change amid structural shifts. Not surprisingly, when we critically examine how structural forces—such as class, co-ethnic networks, and schooling resources—affect parental strategies among Asian American families, we begin to see a different, more complex picture.

When we initially compare the experiences of both groups of Korean American parents, we see many similarities. Each values education, and each wants to send their children to college to provide them more opportunities than they had as first-generation immigrants. Furthermore, because of their confinement to an ethnic economy comprising small family businesses and because of their limited English language skills and knowledge of the U.S. education system, both groups were handicapped in providing their children with direct schooling assistance. In fact, they were at a marked disadvantage compared with native-born, White, middle-class parents, who can often help with their children's homework and engage teachers about their children's schooling.

A closer look at the Korean parents, however, reveals key structural differences between the two groups. The Korean American parents at MH were more likely to have been college-educated professionals in Korea. Although a majority in both groups worked in the ethnic economy, the MH parents were more likely to be businesses owners and middle class, unlike the bulk of the working-class parents or parents of high school dropouts, who usually worked for co-ethnic entrepreneurs. Moreover, the MH parents were less likely to be single parents relying on only one source of income.

Consequently, the MH parents had greater access to social capital for assisting their children in school. By being embedded in strong co-ethnic networks, such as those found in Korean churches, the MH parents were better able to reinforce the value of education in their children, gain important information on schooling, and navigate the school system. Equally important, this group also could translate their shared values and information into school achievement for their children, usually by hiring private bilingual tutors and college counselors as well as by sending their children to private, tuition-based after-school academies in Korean ethnic enclaves. By doing so, they compensated for their limited English skills and the scant bilingual assistance available at their children's school. In providing such structural resources, the MH Korean American parents supported their children in using education as a long-term investment—a family goal that would move their children away from the ethnic economy and toward career opportunities in the mainstream economy.

The Korean parents of high school dropouts, on the other hand, faced numerous structural barriers to accumulating social capital and, therefore, to supporting their children in school. One such barrier was their long working hours, which translated into less parental supervision and guidance at home—this was especially the case for single parents in the group. Another barrier was their income, which curtailed their ability to hire private tutors and counselors or to send their children to after-school academies; instead, they relied solely on inadequate neighborhood public schools for their children's education. Located in poor, urban communities and serving mainly low-income minority children and recent immigrants, the schools were ill equipped to provide either substantial academic support for the children or bilingual assistance for immigrant parents. As a result, some poor and working-class parents resorted to transferring their children to other schools in and outside their neighborhood. Those schools, however, were similarly lacking in resources, and because these children frequently changed schools, they often ended up isolated and alone, devoid of institutional support and further alienated from school. Lacking crucial structural resources, the parents of high school dropouts found it difficult to leverage education as a long-term investment for their children. More often than not, their children's after-school activity of choice—or necessity—was going to work to supplement the family's income, usually at menial jobs in ethnic enclaves, thereby reproducing the low status of their immigrant parents.

As the findings in the following chapters illustrate, Korean American parents and children are hardly a homogeneous group. Despite sharing the value of education, the parents experienced the U.S. education system quite differently as a result of structural factors such as income, network orientation, and school resources. Such variability in accessing and accumulating social capital had important implications, determining how and to what extent the two groups could help their children bridge the gap between schooling aspirations and achievement.

● CHAPTER 2 ●

Magnet High's Korean American Students: Parental and Co-Ethnic Support

> My parents always talk about how important it is to do well in school. They constantly push me to do the best that I can. That's all they want from me, really. They say that education will pay off in the long run.
>
> —Jenny, age 17

PARENTAL EXPECTATIONS: EDUCATION AS A LONG-TERM INVESTMENT

The high-achieving Korean American students at MH placed much faith in education. Throughout the interview period at MH, the students consistently related their parents' educational expectations, while reiterating how education was an effective, if not the only, way to achieve economic mobility. They shared their parents' educational aspirations and, like them, believed in the significance of schooling as a long-term investment that would eventually pay dividends. This direct linkage between schooling and economic mobility was consistently framed in these terms: Achieving academically in high school leads to acceptance at an elite college, which in turn leads to economic and career opportunities.

Kay was an eleventh grader who reiterated her parent's educational aspirations, believing that education was the main way to achieve success in a competitive society. She suggested that one needs education not only to "make it" but also to "survive."

> You know, this world is just getting more demanding. It's like you have to have the better qualification than the next guy. I mean, if you don't have education, you are just not going to make it. I think this world is all a matter of Darwin's theory. You know, only the strong can survive, and so if you want to be something and go out there and get something done, then you got to keep up and actually be informed on top of all that.

Such a firm belief in education was echoed by Esther, who was careful to explain that her Korean and other Asian friends experienced similar parental expectations: "All of my friends who are Asian or Korean, their parents are all strict. They all want their kids to get 99 average and go to good college. . . . They definitely want above average." She continued to outline the direct and strong connection among high school, college, and economic status. "Being successful means getting really good grades and getting into a good college so you don't have to struggle financially, you know. My mom always says that if I study hard, I will have lots of opportunities in the future."

Kay and Esther clearly wanted to excel. Listening closely to the reasons behind their desire, however, we can sense another message, one framed by structural barriers with which the students were all too familiar, having grown up with immigrant parents. In relating their aspirations of education, the MH students consistently referred to their parents' struggles working in the ethnic economy, either as small-business owners or as menial laborers for other entrepreneurs. The long hours, menial work, and unpredictable economic conditions shaped both the parents' and students' outlook. By growing up with immigrant parents who endure such hardships, the MH students learned to view education as a means of gaining career opportunities outside the ethnic economy.

For instance, Jennifer's mother worked as a hairdresser for a Korean business owner. Seeing how her mother worked long hours in menial labor encouraged her to excel in school so that she can pursue career opportunities that yield more income and social status:

> I want education because I don't want to end up as a hairdresser, like my mom, always working with her hands and, like, always tired when I come home. So as long as you have education, you are fine. I am going to work hard like my parents do, but I also want it sort of easier. Since I have education here, it will be easier for me.

In addition to long hours and menial work, students spoke of the financial instability and stress that came with their parents' business. Ted's parents owned a grocery store in Manhattan that was open 24 hours a day, 7 days a week. When he was not too busy with schoolwork, he helped his parents at the store; he noted how hard his parents work. When I asked him if he would ever take over his parents' business, he looked at me in disbelief: "Are you kidding, there is no way! It's a lot of work, and you work all the time. Sometimes business is good, but sometimes it's not. Besides, my parents are working this hard so that I don't have to. And that's why I have to do well in school, so that I have other options." Generally speaking, for Ted and many other students, options meant a career that would afford them a better quality of life, which included enjoying their work and having time to spend with their family and friends. His comment also spoke to the precarious nature of owning a small family business that does not guarantee financial success. As Ted explained:

> I want an easier life than they [his parents] had. I think success for me would be having a job where I would not have to spend all my time doing work, but I would have time to spend with my family. Spend time doing activities that I like to do. Like, music was a big part of my life, so I want that. They don't want me to work as hard—and without so much stress. They want me to give my best, and at the same time enjoy it and have a lot less stress than they did.

The students' accounts of their parents' struggles illustrated the difficult work conditions faced by Korean immigrant entrepreneurs and co-workers. As illustrated, the second-generation Korean Americans at MH are likely to reject such lifelong entrepreneurship and employment in the ethnic economy. The combination of wider opportunities in the mainstream economy and the disincentives to working in the ethnic economy account for this. The findings support studies that show how many first-generation Korean Americans have used entrepreneurship as a way to achieve economic mobility, but this avenue has been largely rejected by middle-class second-generation Korean Americans who are educated and raised in the United States (Abelmann & Lie, 1995; E. Y. Kim, 1993; Kim, 2004; Min, 1998). That is, middle-class second-generation Koreans are choosing career opportunities in the mainstream economy and leaving the ethnic economy behind with their immigrant parents. Although the co-ethnic economy may prove to be an important means of economic mobility for first-generation Korean American immigrants, this avenue may not necessarily be the case for their second-generation children, especially for those who come from middle-class backgrounds.

More than any other Asian American communities, Korean Americans have been noted for their "middle-class" entrepreneurial status and strong co-ethnic networks. Although many were college-educated professionals in Korea, a formidable language barrier restricted most from finding comparable professional jobs in the United States (Light & Bonacich, 1988; Min, 1995, 1996; Park, 1997). As an alternative to blue-collar occupations, many Korean immigrants turned to owning and operating small businesses.

According to a 1986 survey that Min (1995) conducted, approximately 45% of working Korean immigrants in Los Angeles were small-businesses owners (while another 30% found employment in the Korean ethnic enclave). In New York City, this pattern of Korean American entrepreneurship was equally pronounced. In 1992, there were approximately 1,800 Korean-owned green groceries in New York, accounting for some 60% of the total green groceries in the metropolitan area. In addition, a Korean business district in

New York City known as *Hanin Sangga* thrives. Like Los Angeles, New York City has become an overseas Seoul, replete with growing international trade and businesses. Min (1995) reported that in each of the major cities on the eastern seaboard—Boston, New York, Newark, Philadelphia, Baltimore, and Washington, D.C.—there exists a growing number of Korean ethnic businesses, community associations, and Christian churches.

While Korean American entrepreneurship and the ethnic economy have proved beneficial to Korean Americans exploiting this niche, researchers are careful to point out the significance of poverty, racism, and other institutional barriers faced by Korean American communities (Abelmann & Lie, 1995; Hurh & Kim, 1984, 1989; E. H. Kim, 1993; Kim, 1999; Kim, 2000; Kim & Yu, 1996; Min 1996). For one thing, small businesses in Korean ethnic enclaves play the intermediary role of distributing goods produced by the ruling capitalist groups to poor inner-city residents, bridging the status gap between the higher- and lower-class sectors (Light & Bonacich, 1988; Min, 1996). Coined the "middleman minority" group, Korean entrepreneurs, by taking the intermediary role between the producers and minority consumers, have also been subjected to high levels of hostility and rejection, particularly from minority customers (Min, 1996). These conflicts have occurred in all major Korean communities in the United States but have been most severe in New York and Los Angeles. At least five boycott movements have been staged against Korean merchants in New York City since 1981 (Min, 1996). During the 1992 riot in Los Angeles, about 2,300 Korean-owned stores located in South Central Los Angeles and Koreatown were burned or looted. Property damage incurred by Korean small-business owners during the riot was estimated at more than $350 million (Min, 1996). Used as scapegoats to downplay the racial conflict and economic disparity between Blacks and Whites, Korean Americans became targets of the tensions and inequities in the Los Angeles area (Abelmann & Lie, 1995; E. H. Kim, 1993; Kim, 1999; Kim, 2000).

Because of the language barrier, racism, and other structural factors, entrepreneurship for immigrants has historically provided an important alternative to limited primary-sector labor-market opportunities and the daunting prospect of unemployment (Light & Gold, 2000). Korean Americans are no exception: They have resorted to self-employment and strong ethnic networks as important strategies to achieve economic mobility (Kim, 1981; Light & Bonacich, 1988; Min, 1996; Park, 1997; Portes & Rumbaut, 1996, 2001). However, as this research shows, middle-class and socially mobile second-generation Korean Americans are using education as a way to leave behind immigrant parents' family business in order to find economic and professional opportunities outside the ethnic economy.

Despite their parents' educational and professional background, many first-generation Korean immigrants not only work long hours but do so in menial jobs often situated in impoverished urban neighborhoods. Having grown up in this environment, the Korean American students at MH tended to couch their parent's struggles in terms of sacrifice. The time-honored notion of immigrant parents working hard to provide opportunities for their American-born and -raised children held true for the majority of MH students, many of whom not only acknowledged their parents' struggles but believed they should end with them. In keeping with this, the students' career decisions were, in many ways, a practical means of achieving economic and social status not only for themselves but also for their parents (Louie, 2001, 2004; Suárez-Orozco & Suárez-Orozco, 2001).

Ellen was a tenth grader planning to major in economics in college. By drawing a direct relationship among education, college, and economic mobility, she explained the importance of financial security. Like her parents, she believed that being economically stable is an important means of achieving "happiness." When I asked her how she defined being successful, she repeated the conversation she had had with her parents:

> I guess money, because my parents say that if you want to be happy, you need money, you know. A lot of people say that you can't buy happiness with money, and my parents don't think otherwise, but if you think about it, it's partly true. I guess how much respect I get from others, how much others look toward me depends on that.

At the same time, while students wanted to adhere to their parents' wishes of obtaining financial security by becoming the next high-powered lawyers, doctors, and corporate executives, they were also conflicted. Deciphering what they wanted to pursue as a career, versus what their parents thought was best for them, proved difficult. For instance, as an eleventh grader, Kay was preparing to apply to colleges and had thought much about her career options. Although she wanted to be a teacher, her mother wanted her to pursue medicine. Her comments revealed the conflict and confusion that many students faced as they tried to navigate between parental expectations and their own interests and dreams:

> For a long time, I've listened to my mom. But now, I am trying to figure out what I want. I am confused if it's what she wants or what I want. I want to teach, but my mom thinks that it doesn't pay enough. I try to avoid talking to her about this stuff. You know, I say, "OK," but then I go into my room. I feel like she puts a double standard. She says she wants me to become a doctor but then at the same time tells me to do what I want.

While such conflict arises for many students, it plays out as the reverse for others. For instance, unlike Kay's mother, Janice's parents encouraged her to attend college and choose a career she would enjoy. Consequently, Janice experienced less conflict from parental expectations:

> Well, I know that doing well in school and going to a good college is supposed to be for me, but I want them [her parents] to be proud of me. It's how much effort I put into it. They want me to go to college, and they want me to have a good career . . . anything that I would enjoy doing. They want me to have fun and have friends.

Because Janice's parents did not use their sacrifice to influence her career choice, Janice was free to appreciate her parents' sacrifice more fully, to the point where she wanted to actively please them. To be sure, both Janice and Kay wanted to repay their parents' sacrifice by making them proud, but the autonomy given to Janice meant less inner conflict and turmoil for her.

Actual career choices aside, the MH students were clear about parental expectations and the effect a college education has on career options. The students firmly believed that education would afford them career opportunities outside the ethnic economy, which would yield a higher salary, status, and quality of life than what they had experienced growing up with immigrant parents. From the students' perspective, there was a clear link among excelling in high school, attending a competitive college, and obtaining career opportunities, with academic achievement in high school being an important step toward a long-term trajectory of economic and social mobility.

PARENTAL STRATEGIES: CLASS, SOCIAL CAPITAL, AND SCHOOLING RESOURCES

To help their children use education as a long-term investment and turn their schooling aspirations into actual achievement, the MH parents had to provide them with important structural and educational resources. To this end, the MH parents actively intervened in their children's schooling and adopted the following strategies: (1) using their kinship and co-ethnic networks at church, work, and communities to reinforce the values of education, bilingual skills, and ethnic ties; (2) using co-ethnic networks to gain important schooling information necessary for navigating the public school system; (3) sending their children to tuition-based after-school academies, located predominately in Korean ethnic enclaves, in order to support their children academically and prepare them for college; (4) hiring private bilingual tutors and counselors to compensate for the parents' limited English language skills and knowledge of the U.S. education system as well as to intervene in the children's schooling and college admissions process.

These strategies highlight the importance of structural resources and their relationship to school achievement. While the Korean American MH students' values—their belief in and faith in education—may explain why they strive in school, they only partially account for why the children might succeed. For these values to translate into school achievement, important structural and institutional support from families, communities, and schools must be present. Equipped with higher socioeconomic backgrounds and access to social capital, the Korean parents at MH were more likely than their YCC counterparts to assist their children in translating educational aspirations into concrete academic achievement.

ROLE OF THE KOREAN CHURCH: REINFORCING VALUES OF EDUCATION, LANGUAGE, AND ETHNIC TIES

When I first began my research at Magnet High, several teachers enthusiastically offered advice on how to identify and locate Korean American students for the interviews: "If you find one Korean American student, she or he will lead you to all the others." Throughout the months at Magnet High, I learned that, indeed, many Korean American students not only knew each other from the school but had been friends before entering Magnet High, usually because they belonged to the same co-ethnic churches or community organizations. In some cases, the students sought out specific Korean American peers when they entered Magnet High because their parents and siblings were members of the same Korean church.

Mary and Kim had been acquaintances at the same Korean church for 5 years. Now that they were in the same high school, they were becoming even closer friends and spoke fondly about their church experiences. When I asked them why their families went to Korean churches, Mary proudly spoke of the social and religious support that the ethnic church provided for her family. She explained that because she had been attending the same church with her parents since she was a child, her parents' church friends represented an extended or surrogate family. She explained that her parents attended church not only for religious reasons but also for the meaningful friendships that develop there, connections akin to familial relations:

> My dad is involved in choir and church. My parents look for not somebody they can just gossip with and discuss the newest video or what just happened in Korea, but basically bonding and being like a family because we don't really have family here. Well, we do, but they are in Ohio and California and not near the area, so my parents look to their friends for bonding and being sort of like a surrogate family and being an extended family.

The Korean American parents at MH gained many forms of economic and social support from their co-ethnic networks, and the networks that mattered most sprang from Korean church, where the Korean parents and their children came together regularly. This is not surprising, given the large number of Christians in Korean American communities. Although Christians constitute only about 20% of the population in Korea, almost 75% of Korean American adult immigrants attend Korean ethnic churches, most of them Protestant (Kim, 1977; Kim, 1981; Kwon et al., 2001; Min, 1995, 1996). As mentioned previously, a large segment of Korean émigrés to the United States are Christian, and many who had no affiliation with Christianity prior to emigrating attend ethnic churches here in order to maintain ties to other Koreans, to take advantage of cultural and social service programs, and to gain social and linguistic support. For a disproportionately large number of Korean immigrant families, ethnically rooted churches not only serve as religious centers but also become social and cultural centers that provide valuable support (Kwon et al., 2001).

The Korean American students at MH corroborated this, reiterating that their parents attended co-ethnic church with their children for religious and cultural reasons, as a way to teach their American-born and -raised children the significance of learning the Korean language, culture, and history. Many students conveyed their experience of having attended the same Korean church with their parents since childhood and of how adult members—parents, friends, and ministers—upheld and reinforced the importance of excelling in school, the importance of maintaining the Korean language and ethnic consciousness, and the overall values of students' immigrant parents. Ultimately, the social capital found within Korean churches reinforced shared norms and ties to ethnic networks at home, in communities, and in school.

Take the case of Samantha, a ninth grader born in the United States. Having attended the same Korean church with her parents since she could remember, she explained the importance of learning the Korean language so that she could better communicate with her parents and maintain close ties with her Korean community. To that end, she actively participated in what she referred to as a "Korean" youth group, run by first-generation church members speaking Korean. Her church also had an "English" youth group run by second-generation church members using English, but she chose the former so that she could continue to practice and maintain her Korean language skill.

> We are, like, devoted Christians. We always go to church and stuff, and, like, if there is a festival during Thanksgiving, like, people from Korea come, and we always go to those. I think they [her parents] go because, partly, they want to show us more about our culture, since we are in America. They go to Korean church because they don't speak very good English . . . well, in my church there is different

youth groups. There's a Korean youth group and an English youth group, and it was my choice to go to Korean. Since I am Korean, I think it's better that you learn to speak Korean and could speak it with parents and friends and stuff, so to enforce that, I kind of went to the Korean youth group. And there were people that I knew who went to Korean. English youth group is very Americanized. They speak more English than Korean. Ours is all Korean, and since I understand Korean, too, and I don't want to, like, go away from my culture and stuff, so I wanted to stick to it.

When I asked students "What messages do you get from your parents and their friends in Korean churches?" they explained that Korean parents expected not only academic achievement but for them to attend competitive colleges and speak the Korean language. As one student commented, "A lot of Korean parents want their kids to get good grades, go to Ivy League colleges, speak fluent Korean, and be proud of being Korean. Parents are similar in how they think. The parents want all the students to go to the best colleges and after-school programs, and all the parents are traditional. A lot of Korean parents expect these things from their kids."

These comments support findings of earlier studies on post-1965 second-generation children, which depict how strong social networks among immigrant communities reinforce the value of education and attitudes that are conducive to academic success (Portes & Rumbaut, 1996, 2001; Waters, 1999; Zhou & Bankston, 1996, 1998). In her ethnographic study of Black West Indian immigrants in New York, Waters (1999) found that ethnically rooted churches provided important social support for the immigrant communities. She argued that networks within ethnic church reinforced ties between immigrant parents and their children, while reinforcing certain values such as hard work, family, and education. Second-generation children who belonged to these ethnically rooted churches maintained close ties with their immigrant parents and other ethnic adults. This reinforcement of ethnic ties and identities not only helped second-generation children to achieve academically but also helped insulate them from the stratifying forces of poverty and racism endemic to their impoverished neighborhoods.

By attending Korean churches with their parents and maintaining close ties to their parental networks, the Korean American students at MH were part of what Coleman and Hoffer (1987) referred to as a "closed functional community," one in which social networks provide children with access to multiple sets of "parents" who reinforce the same values and attitudes that are conducive to school success. In addition, resources that parents lack can potentially be gained from other members of the community. Put another way, closed functional communities merge the public and private spheres, encouraging adult peers in both private and public spaces to sanction common norms that guide children's behaviors and activities. What we come to understand, ultimately, is that conformity to norms and expectations in a social network is an important attribute of social capital. The high-achieving Korean American students at MH understood this well, subject as they were to multiple sources of social pressure to succeed in school. "The strengths of these relations and the pressure they can exert on a young person are exceedingly great, which implies that they constitute an extraordinarily powerful form of social capital" (Coleman & Hoffer, 1987, p. 236).

However, this social capital, in turn, produces ancillary effects. In fact, the MH students' accounts also reveal how social pressure to excel in school results in fierce competition with and obligation to other members of the ethnic community. This prompted marked emotional responses in the students, especially when their parents compared their academic achievement and placed the families in competition with one another. For instance, Mary related her conflicted emotions about being embedded in a co-ethnic community, where those who achieve academically and speak fluent Korean are most revered within their parents' first-generation circle.

> My father has many Korean friends. They would come over and come to each other's houses, and we talk, children are compared of their smartness or something. "Oh, my son goes to Stuyvesant," "Oh, my daughter goes to Bronx Science," "Oh, my son will be the captain of the tennis team," "My daughter is really well-rounded student; she is on the debate team," or something like that. I just sit there and, like, OK. All I do is smile and nod.

Such competition over academic achievement continues beyond the students' high school years. Many of them conveyed how their parents often compared which colleges their children attended and which professional careers they pursued. As one student commented:

> Usually, if Korean parents see that you go to a good college, one parent would say, "My child goes to Harvard," and the other parent would say, "My child goes to NYU" and "He is a doctor, lawyer, or whatever." It's like they compare other people's children.

When I asked my informants how they dealt with such competition, some expressed resentment and anger toward their parents and co-ethnic adults. One student confessed, "It makes me feel like an object, like something that you show off." Some also revealed that in their effort to please their parents, they resorted to lying about their school grades. For instance, Laura remarked how she had to lie to her parents about her grades because she was unable to achieve the perfect score that her mother expected. When her mother's pressure became too great for her to bear, Laura spoke openly about her academic standing and resisted her mother's expectations:

> She [mother] wants me to get 100's all the time. And grades, grades, grades, that's all she cares about. In freshman year, I did so bad, I couldn't even show her my report card. I lied and said that this year they are not sending report cards, but then starting sophomore year, I started showing it to her and said this is what I could do, so she started accepting it. When she forced me in freshman year, I didn't do so well. I started doing better when she started letting me do it myself. I know when I should study and not study. I know she cares, but I don't like being forced.

Adding to the students' pressure was an awareness that school performance and family reputation were linked. The Korean American students at MH consistently conveyed that school achievement was important not only for their personal gain but also for their parents and family. How parents were perceived by their co-ethnic peers hinged, in part, on how their children performed in school. Students firmly believed that their grades and test scores became a litmus test for their parents child rearing. Samantha explained:

> When I think of my parents, I think how much they want from me and expect from me. It will be seen as a failure on my parents' part not to raise me properly if I don't get that A.

These comments support other studies showing how children of immigrants see academic success not only as an avenue of individual mobility but also as a way to bring honor or success to their immigrant families (Gibson, 1988; Hsu, 1971; Sung, 1987). Conversely, my informants' responses revealed that to fall short of these normative standards and expectations was to bring shame upon their families and face the possibility of social exclusion.

It is also interesting to note that such social expectations and comparisons were not always unidirectional from parents to children. For instance, as parents compared their children's academic achievements, the Korean students at MH also compared their parents' child rearing and expectations, including their curfews and disciplinary measures. In effect, by reenacting this ritual and holding their parents' performances up to scrutiny against community norms, the students reversed roles with their parents. In the process, they learned to gauge whether their parents' expectations were reasonable or worth contesting. Susan, a tenth grader at MH, explained:

> As long as she [Susan's mother] is like other mothers, the way that other mothers are, I would listen, I would have no question about it,

> 'cause I would know that other Korean parents are like that, so what can I expect? How can I tell her not to tell me to do something that other parents tell their kids? As long as she is like other parents and all other typical parents, then I would listen to her. I would have no question about her.

In this complex and multidimensional process, the MH parents and their children mutually reinforced the values inherent in their social networks. In other words, they both acted within the norms of the network, using them as a barometer by which to judge each other's behavior.

By including their children in their co-ethnic networks, ultimately the MH parents were able to effectively sanction their values of education, family, and the Korean language, which in turn reinforced their children's ethnic and familial ties. The strength of these social relationships within the network came from their degree of intensity, level of trust, frequency of intimacy, reciprocity, and acknowledged obligations (Granovetter, 1985; Lin, 2000). The stronger these relationships within networks, the more likely that the sharing and exchanging of resources occur, where both collective and individual actors invest in social relations to protect their existing resources and to gain additional ones (Lin, 2000, p. 47).

SCHOOLING INFORMATION AND SUPPORT

Elite Public High Schools

One of the more important sets of resources to be gained from having access to social capital is flow of information about choices and opportunities that can be used for a purposeful action (Lin, 2000). For instance, by being embedded in strong social networks in their communities, the parents at MH learned how to navigate the public school system, gain information on private after-school programs, and hire private bilingual tutors and counselors for their children. These parental strategies, in part, compensated for their limited English skills and knowledge of the U.S. education system. Moreover, these strategies, which included using their personal funds to provide bilingual assistance, also compensated for the limited bilingual resources available for parents at MH and in the school system in general.

When I first met John, he had only been at MH for a few months. As a newly admitted freshman, he was trying to learn his way around the school and get to classes on time. Although he may have been new to the school, he had known about MH since he was in elementary school, when his parents told him about it. He explained that his parents learned about MH, and how to apply to other elite high schools, through their friends at work. After his arrival at MH, John's parents also told his uncle about the application process. John's cousin eventually followed in his footsteps:

> My parents expected me to apply to this high school since I was in elementary school. They heard about it through their friends at work, and then they told my uncle and aunt. Now my cousins are applying this year.

The clear impetus for applying to MH and other elite public high schools was the free tuition and their academic reputation. Conversely, the parents believed that if their children did not make it to one of the specialized high schools, they would have to attend one of the poor-quality public schools in their neighborhood. Given the outstanding reputation of the elite magnet high schools, the limited choice of quality public schools available to them in their respective urban neighborhoods, and their inability to send their children to an elite private high school because of limited funds, many MH parents felt that it was extremely important for their children to gain admission to one of the specialized public high schools.

When I met her, Kimberly was a 17-year-old junior preparing to apply to college. She was admitted to MH as a freshman and had come there from a middle school comprised of mostly poor, minority children. She explained that had she not been admitted to MH, she would have had to resort to the public high school in her neighborhood—a gloomy prospect for her and her parents. Although she was relieved to have been accepted at MH, she recalled the experience of her cousin, who was not so fortunate:

> I learned about the specialized high schools through my cousin. She went through it before me, so I learned through her experience. She applied but didn't make it. She went to her local high school but eventually dropped out. My parents now think all local high schools are terrible, and that they make you into gangsters. My other cousin went to another public high school because he didn't get in, and he didn't turn out that good. So, my parents think that specialized high school is good and [are] glad that I got in.

In their research on second-generation children in New York City, Kasinitz, Mollenkopf, Waters, Lopez, and Kim (1997) found that Chinese American interviewees took advantage of the best that the New York public school system afforded, despite their low socioeconomic status and limited English skills. The study indicated that, while none of the Chinese interviewees had attended private or parochial schools, many had attended elite magnet schools. As a result of strong co-ethnic networks among the first-generation parents, students were able to access important information about the elite public schools and gain entrance to them. The interviewees in the study benefited from high degrees of economic concentration among their first-generation parents as well as lower degrees of residential segregation. Ultimately, strong first-generation co-ethnic networks helped the second-generation interviewees learn about elite magnet high schools and take advantage of the public school system. Furthermore, how the children of immigrants learned to maneuver within the public school systems had enormous impact on second-generation educational outcome.

Private After-School Academies and Bilingual Tutors and Counselors

In addition to elite public high schools, the Korean parents learned about private after-school programs in Korean ethnic enclaves. These privately run, tuition-based after-school academies, called *hagwon*, offer cram classes that prepare students for standardized exams, learn Korean and English language skills, and reinforce other academic disciplines. Many parents at MH sent their children to *hagwon* to help them prepare for college entrance exams and get ahead in their schoolwork (Kao, 1995; Schneider & Lee, 1990; Zhou, 1997).

During the summer, Alice attended *hagwon* in Flushing, Queens, to prepare for the SAT I and II exams; she knew that when school started in the fall, she would not have as much time to study. To illustrate why she attended this private academy, she repeated her conversations with her parents. Noting their parents' portrayal of the Korean education system, Alice explained how high school students in Korea attend *hagwon* in order to do well on a competitive college entrance exam—reflecting a process that is more difficult and strenuous than what she has to endure in the United States. Even though Alice was born and raised in the United States and had never attended school in Korea, she used the Korean education system as a point of reference:

> My parents send me to *hagwon* so I can do better on SAT and stuff. I go to *hagwon* during the summer, too, so that I can prepare for school. I wouldn't try as hard if my parents were not pushing me. They say that it's really hard in Korea, and students go to *hagwon*, study really hard there. In Korea, it's so strict . . . they expect me to do the same.

According to the MH students, their parents often used the Korean education system as a point of reference in educating their children in the United States. For instance, in Korea it is common for, if not expected of, students to attend *hagwon* as early as kindergarten. As in the United States, these private, tuition-based after-school academies provide additional tutoring to help children excel in school and prepare for competitive high school and college entrance exams. However, these private after-school academies, both in Korea and the United States, usually emphasize rote memorization, test-taking skills, and cram methods specifically geared toward improving test scores. As profit-generating businesses designed primarily to improve standardized test scores, these academies rarely provide enriching curriculum for cognitive development based on progressive teaching methods and pedagogy.

According to a recent survey conducted in Korea, it is estimated that an overwhelming 83.1% of elementary school students, 75.3% of middle school students, and 56.4% of high school students attend *hagwon* after school ("Public Education Crisis," 2003). A survey published by a state-run education research institute highlighted the problem associated with this trend, which includes staggering financial burdens on families, as well as parents' lack of confidence in the public education system, which they claim is failing them. It is estimated that families spent 13.64 trillion won ($22.5 billion) on private tutoring in 2003. That amounts to 2.3% of the 2002 gross domestic product, or 55% of the government education budget in 2003 ("Public Education Crisis," 2003). It is reported that parents are putting pressure on the government to reform its public school system so it is less dependent on these private profit-seeking enterprises. Meanwhile, the number of private *hagwon* academies has been rapidly increasing throughout the country, as students are expected to put in longer hours studying and parents are expected to shoulder greater financial burden, often starting as soon as their children reach kindergarten ("Public Education Crisis," 2003).

The MH immigrant parents' inclination to use the Korean education system as a point of reference to educate their children in the United States illustrates the significance of their pre- *and* post-immigration social status (Hirschman & Wong, 1986; Kasinitz, Mollenkopf, & Waters, 2004; Portes & Rumbaut, 1996, 2001). On the one hand, this tendency reflects a pattern of amassing cultural capital derived from their status as college-educated professionals in Korea. Witness their active intervention in their children's schooling by sending them to *hagwon* and by hiring private tutors and counselors. On the other hand, their orientation reflects their relatively low status as U.S. immigrants. With the exception of a few MH parents who attended graduate school in the United States, they often had little understanding of the workings and logistics of high school curricula or of the U.S. college admission process, and they were at a disadvantage in directly assisting their children with schoolwork, college counseling, and career opportunities outside of their ethnic economy.

Repeatedly, MH students described how their immigrant parents—given their own lack of U.S. education, not to mention their language and cultural barriers—were unable to directly offer concrete schooling support or advice on college admissions. Most students explained that even though their parents recognized the names of elite schools and colleges, by and large they could not provide concrete daily schooling support. In fact, many students noted that teaching their parents about the U.S. education system usually falls to them.

Paul, a 16-year-old sophomore born in the United States, confirmed this sense of simultaneous recognition and helplessness on the part of many Korean immigrant parents, who push their children to study hard and to do their best without being able to give them direct and concrete advice on *how* to excel in school:

> My parents could not help me in school because school and education in high school today is too much for them. I mean, a lot of the kids come into school with poor immigrant parents, and they don't even know what the hell their kids are doing. I think basically, like, parents say do your work, try your best, that kind of thing . . . but it's difficult for most parents to help because they are not even sure what or how they can help except by pushing them.

Some students were careful to point out that their parents' English skills were good enough to help them early in their school careers at the elementary level and shortly thereafter. However, since they had entered high school, their parents' English skills were not sophisticated enough to enable them to help their children with subjects like history, English, or biology. As such, the students are often the ones to educate their parents on school-related topics. Minnie was a 17-year-old junior in the midst of applying to colleges when I interviewed her. She described her frustration at having to teach her parents about various college exams and the application process:

> In elementary and junior high school, my parents used to know every test that I had, but now I told them I have to take SAT II, and they say, "What is SAT II?" You know, they don't know anything, so, like, that's probably why they don't bother talking to me about anything—that's why they don't push me to do anything like that, because they are not familiar with, like, what kind of testing there are, how we learn in school.

These comments illustrate how, unlike many middle-class White parents, Korean American MH parents struggle with providing direct schooling support to their children. Since the family members of White, middle-class students often have connections to mainstream institutional resources and opportunities, the parents themselves often act as valuable institutional gatekeepers who negotiate the transmission of institutional resources and opportunities for their children (Boykin, 1986; Lareau, 1987, 2003; Phelan et al., 1993; Stanton-Salazar, 1997, 2001).

In any case, another key strategy MH parents used to compensate for their limited ability to directly assist their children was to spend personal funds on private bilingual tutors and college counselors. Kay was a MH junior busily preparing for college exams when I interviewed her. Although she could have sought a college counselor at her public magnet high school, she preferred to consult with a private Korean college counselor because of the personal attention that she received. She explained how the Korean college counselor hired by her parents helped her with the application process and provided college counseling advice:

> I have Ms. B [school counselor], but I've only seen her once, and never again. My parents got me a Korean college counselor, and we've been meeting with him. My parents' friends knew of the counselor, and a lot of people from this school go to him. He knows what standards are for students to specific colleges. He does everything . . . he does the college process, tells us what SAT scores I need, which college is most suitable, financial aids, and deadlines. He will proofread college essays.

In addition to providing students with personalized advice on college exams and the application process, many of these private counselors proved an invaluable bilingual and bicultural asset to the parents, helping them compensate for MH's limited bilingual outreach. The scope of the problem was illustrated by Kay, who explained how the language barrier hampered her parents as well as many of her MH friends' parents—for instance, few parents attended open-school nights or readily spoke to the children's teachers. What followed was a win–win scenario. The private bilingual counselors mitigated the situation by helping Kay's and other parents to be more involved in their children's schooling, and the students gained not only private counseling but also a way to include their parents in their school and college application process. Kay continued:

> Teachers in the school and students should have a tighter relationship, but it's hard to find a teacher who will go out of the way to do things for you. It helps that he [Korean counselor] is also Korean, because he can understand what is good for me and my parents. He meets with my parents and me separately, and then meets us together. He tells me what my parents want me to do, and then tells me what he thinks I should do. And it's good because he can communicate with my parents better than a White person.

Ultimately, the MH parents, by resorting to *hagwon*, compensated for two limitations: their own and the magnet high school's. They acquired schooling assistance for their children that neither could provide, mainly by leveraging strong social networks, sending their children to private after-school programs, and hiring private tutors and counselors. Consequently, the Korean American students at MH were better prepared than the Korean American high school dropouts for the U.S. educational system, which places a premium on standardized exams and high-stakes testing as a way of measuring student achievement and potential. Furthermore, because many of the private tutors and counselors were bilingual, with experiences of attending schools in the United States and working in the mainstream economy, they were able to act as key institutional agents to provide resources available outside of the immigrant parents' ethnic enclave, as will become more evident in Part II. Thus it is important to highlight the importance of schooling resources available in and outside of immigrant networks when accounting for educational achievement among children of immigrants.

The strategies employed by MH parents also afforded their children assistance with important resources that students need in order to achieve academically. What's important to remember is that these parental strategies were predicated on the parents' social and economic resources. While the MH parents held high educational expectations for their children, they also had the financial capital necessary to translate aspirations into school achievement and help the students pursue education as a long-term investment for economic mobility. The students, in turn, adopted their parents' value of education, often predicated on pre- and post immigrant experience, believing that by excelling in school they would gain higher occupational status than that of their immigrant parents, many of whom could not pursue careers in the United States on a par with their educational level because of their limited English skills. From the perspective of the MH students and parents, investment in education meant gaining career opportunities to move away from menial labor in the ethnic economy and to leave their small family businesses behind. The children internalized these values and aspired to achieve academically as a way to fulfill this long-term goal, not only for themselves but also for their families.

CHAPTER 3

Korean American High School Dropouts: Alone and Isolated

> My parents are very hardworking people. My dad is a construction worker; he works 13 hours a day and 7 days a week. My mom doesn't work because she has to take care of all seven of us. She stays home, she cooks, does laundry, gets important calls for my dad's business. I know what my dad does to put a roof over our heads and what my mom does to take care of us. I know all this, and I still can't do well in school. I always tried but I couldn't.
>
> —Helen, age 18

PARENTAL EXPECTATIONS: LIMITATIONS OF CO-ETHNIC SUPPORT

Helen was an 18-year-old Korean American who immigrated to the United States with her parents when she was less than a year old. In an essay she wrote for her GED class, she described her family's economic struggles as well as her own struggle in school despite her aspirations to achieve. At one point, she explained how her father, who did not graduate from high school, wanted her to excel in school in order to gain more career opportunities. "My dad said that since he is a construction worker and he didn't finish high school, we got to become something better. His only dream is that all of us becoming something that can make a difference in the world." She concluded, "I just hope that there are more good things waiting to happen in the future."

Like their counterparts at Magnet High, the Korean American high school dropouts in this study had been exposed to high parental educational aspirations and knew that education was important. Yet consistently there was a wide gap between parental aspirations and the children's achievement, because the latter were more likely than the MH students to face numerous structural and institutional barriers to gaining important schooling support. Unlike the MH students, who were embedded in strong social networks at home and in their communities, the dropouts consistently spoke of being alone and isolated at home and in school. They repeatedly mentioned having to "take care" of school, career, and financial decisions on their own. Comments such as "There's nobody I can turn to—I am by myself" were common among the students.

Born in the United States, Eugene was 18 years old at the time of this study. Although his baseball cap covered his eyes and cast a dark shadow on his small face, he beamed with a warm smile as I thanked him for agreeing to the interview. Eugene and his widowed, still-single mother had moved to New York City from the Midwest to be near her extended family for economic support. His mother later left the city to look for work and no longer resided in the same household, leaving Eugene to depend for support on his aunt and uncle, with whom he lived. When I asked whether he spoke with his aunt and uncle regarding schooling and career decisions, he explained that he had no one to turn to. Eventually, Eugene decided to drop out of high school, deliberating for some time before doing so. It was a decision that he made mostly on his own, without much adult guidance:

> It took me a month to decide, and it was really hard. Four years, you know, down the drain. My uncle and aunt don't even know I dropped out of high school. . . . They asked me, "Aren't you graduating this year?" And I said, "I will do what I have to do to graduate. You will be satisfied with that, right?" And she said, "Yeah." And so, I decided to take the GED. I dropped out in January.

Eugene's account was typical of the stories told by many of the Korean American high school dropouts, who faced myriad structural barriers to developing networks and forming relationships with adults who could provide crucial support toward their schooling achievement and career opportunities.

To be sure, a majority of the Korean American parents in both the MH and dropout groups worked long hours in menial jobs in the ethnic economy. Growing up with these immigrant parents, both groups of students were at a loss for educational guidance at home and school. But the high school dropouts were more likely to come from households with lower socioeconomic backgrounds, single mothers, and less parental supervision at home. The single mothers, in particular, not only worked for co-ethnic entrepreneurs as waitresses, manicurists, or hairdressers but often had to travel outside the city to obtain work with them. This translated into longer commutes, and they sometimes resorted to leaving their children with relatives as a result. Moreover, because of limited family income, many Korean American high school dropouts themselves had little option but to work after school. All of these structural factors limited the amount of time and resources that the working-class Korean parents, especially single mothers, could contribute to their children's schooling. They also cut into the time the students themselves could devote to their studies.

Ellen was a U.S.-born 18-year-old who had been out of high school for more than a year when I met her. Since her parents' divorce, her mother had had to work 7 days a week as a manicurist for a Korean entrepreneur—although, to be sure, the family had struggled financially ever since she could remember. Ellen explained that while she was in high school, her mother was never home because of her demanding work schedule. She rarely spoke to her mother about schooling or problems she was having. After dropping out of high school, she started working two jobs. "My relationship with my mom is not good. When I dropped out, we fought every day. She wanted me to go to high school. She would say that back in her day, it was really hard to go to college, and she is suffering right now because she didn't graduate college." She continued, "I want to get my GED, but I also have to work to make a living. Since I left school, I've been working full time as a manicurist and a receptionist at an office." She found that in contrast to school, where she was failing and was "getting into trouble," working afforded her financial independence and resulted in a "better use of time."

An overwhelming number of studies have shown that high school dropouts in general are more likely to come from families of low socioeconomic status (SES) headed by parents who are unable to be actively involved in their children's schooling because of long working hours and limited access to structural resources (Dornbusch et al., 1985; Duncan & Hoffman, 1985; Ekstrom, Goertz, Pollack, & Rock, 1986; Furstenberg, Gunn, & Morgan, 1987; Natriello, McDill, & Pallos, 1990; Rumberger, Ghatak, Poulos, Ritter, & Dornbusch, 1990). In particular, children raised by single mothers are more vulnerable to poverty because women typically earn lower wages than men and have less job experience because of childbearing and child rearing (Duncan & Hoffman, 1985; Pong & Ju, 2000). This precarious economic status greatly diminishes these mothers' ability to be actively involved in their children's schooling, thereby contributing to the likelihood of high dropout rates among these students (Amato, 1987; Astone & McLananhan, 1991, 1994; Krein & Beller, 1988; McLanahan, 1985). Furthermore, as Pong and Ju (2000) have found, divorce or separation increases the risk of children dropping out, given the emotional, psychological, and economic hardships placed on them. The deep emotional scars and strained relationships with parents often result in alienation and disengagement from home and school.

One of my interviewees, Adam, immigrated to the United States at age 11. He compared his experience growing up in Korea with his experience in the United States, explaining that his mother had been less involved in his schooling here because of her full-time work schedule and limited English skills. "In Korea, my father worked and mother stayed home. But here they both have to work. When I see my Korean friends, I would say 80 to 90% of mothers work. So, my mom was never home because of work, and because they didn't speak English, they were not as involved as they were in Korea.

So they knew, but they couldn't do much." When I asked him how his parents dealt with his dropping out of high school, he replied, "They were not happy at all. They didn't want me to appear less than others in society. They wanted me to stay in school and pushed me a lot, but they were working and busy, so it was difficult."

Because their circumstances forced them to work weekends, many of the dropout parents were also less likely to participate with their children in shared activities such as Korean church, which otherwise might have provided them with important forms of social capital. Therefore, parental messages regarding value of education and the significance of a college degree were not as effective as they were for MH students, who were embedded in strong networks with parents and their adult friends.

Furthermore, as I will explain in the following section, when the dropouts did attend Korean church, they usually associated with Korean American youths also from low-income families, many of whom were high school dropouts or bound for the military. Their association with other low-income Korean Americans meant they gained access to the type of information tailored to their specific needs—information on short-term jobs, GED programs, and joining the military. Although this was certainly helpful for the dropouts, it was starkly different from what was passed on to the MH students, ultimately preparing the former for lower-status positions in the mainstream economy that they might one day move into. That is, the Korean American high school dropouts adopted a different network orientation, operating from a lower hierarchical position and network location.

It is important to point out that while the MH students spoke predominantly about sharing educational aspirations with their immigrant parents, the dropouts spoke readily about the differences and cultural gaps they experienced with theirs. Consequently, instead of conforming to parental expectations and community norms, the high school dropouts actively resisted their parents' educational aspirations as a way to adapt to structural barriers they faced at school and society at large. They were far more likely to adopt an oppositional cultural frame of reference from their peers at school and in their community.

Myung was a 17-year-old who had dropped out of his neighborhood high school the year before I interviewed him. I asked him whether he had ever talked with his parents about schooling and career decisions. He took a deep breath and looked away. After a few minutes, he looked down and began to speak: "You know, we don't really talk. We are very different." He explained that his parents had rarely given him any concrete advice about schooling or jobs but had expected him to do well in school. "All they say is study. But they don't know anything about the schools here, and they can't help me in schools anyways." Then he looked up at me and continued, "But, then, I was really rebellious. Since I've dropped out of high school, they've been better about trying to understand what a teenager goes through. They learned that they can't force me to do things."

Myung's comments illustrate how dropping out of school was both a way to resist his parents' unrealistic demands and an act of defiance that would gain their attention—a call for help and a chance to be heard. Many of the students I interviewed dropped out of high school despite knowing that education was important, explaining repeatedly that their parents' expectations of school success seemed unreasonable and unrealistic. They reiterated the contradiction that existed in their homes: Their parents expected academic achievement but did not provide them with appropriate social and economic support.

Additionally, given the strained relationship with their parents or adults in their extended family, many of my informants were not able to give ready examples of discussions they had had with their parents or guardians about education, future plans, or the kinds of careers they aspired to. The students failed to concretely bridge the gap between the benefits of education and the perceived opportunity structure. When asked to name people they deemed successful, either they could not point to people or, if they did, the individuals were often engaged in menial or dead-end jobs.

During the summer of 2002, I met Alex at the community organization where he was preparing to take the GED. He was a quiet and thoughtful young man who had dropped out of an urban high school in Queens 2 years earlier and was currently unemployed. When I asked him about his relationship with his parents, he stressed the language and cultural barriers between him and his parents and explained that he just stopped communicating with them once he entered high school:

> I don't look up to my parents. I think they work hard, so I like that about them, but we are very different. Our views are very different. It's like, there is nobody I can look up to. No peers, no friends, no counselors or teachers.

Although most of the Korean American dropouts admitted that education was important, they resisted their parents' aspirations as a way to adapt to academic failure and structural limitations. They argued that they dropped out of high school not because they could't achieve in school but because they willingly chose not to. As one student, Chul Shin, explained,

> Education is important. It's what you want to do with it. It's also Korean culture, right? Korean parents, all they think about is education. My son gots [*sic*] to graduate high school, college, you know. I

> didn't want to go to high school, because they wanted me to. I dropped out of high school, not because I couldn't do it, but I didn't want to do it, you know.

If research has shown a strong correlation between family structure and dropout rates, noting that high school dropouts are more likely to come from low-SES families in which parents are less involved in their children's education and decision making, some studies are also careful to point out that indicators of parental involvement vary widely across research. For instance, Sui-Chu and Willms (1996) have argued that some of the emerging studies fail to distinguish between various dimensions of parental involvement. They specifically note that parents' active discussion of school-related activities at home had the strongest effect on their children's school achievement. They found little evidence that lower-SES parents are necessarily *less* involved in their children's schooling than are higher-SES parents. That is, it may be important to also address the kinds of parental involvement and patterns of strategies implemented in families of different social and economic backgrounds, rather than degrees of parental involvement per se.

For instance, Lareau (2003) found that middle-class parents, given their higher occupational status as well as greater access to important cultural capital at home, work, and schools, engaged in a pattern of "concerted cultivation" (p. 38) that provided important institutional support for their children. She found that middle-class parents provided their children with highly structured educational activities that helped them learn academic skills and cultural discourses—a process that further helped them excel in and outside of school. On the other hand, while the working-class parents also have educational aspirations for their children, they did not readily provide such structured educational activities, a result of time and economic limitations and an inability to mobilize their cultural capital into institutional resources for their children's schooling. As such, working-class parents often resorted to "free-play" (nonstructured) child rearing, while relying more on the teachers and schools to take care of their children's schooling (2003).

PARENTAL STRATEGIES: RELYING ON PUBLIC SCHOOLS

Although both groups of Korean parents tried to instill the value of education in their children, they used different strategies—a process that greatly depended on the economic and social resources available to them. As illustrated in the previous section, because they had access to social capital, the magnet high school parents were more likely to reinforce the value of education and to acquire important schooling information for their children. They were also financially able to convert this information into concrete structural support for their children, such as sending them to private, tuition-based educational programs in Korean ethnic enclaves.

By contrast, the working-class Korean American parents, with their low SES and minimal access to social capital, were less likely to effectively reinforce the value of education, acquire schooling information from co-ethnic networks, and translate the information into concrete schooling support for their children. Instead, they adopted different educational strategies, which included (1) turning predominantly to the children's public schools to take care of their children's education and (2) transferring their children from one public high school to another for multiple reasons. In some cases, parents simply wanted to provide their children with a better education. In others, they sought a different schooling environment to remedy their failing grades. Finally, financial circumstances forced some of the families to move to a different school district. In the end, the result was high transfer rate among the Korean high school dropouts that ultimately worked against them.

As resourceful as these parents were, their strategies fell far short of those employed by the MH parents and left their children at a disadvantage when it came to school achievement. For instance, the public high schools that the working-class Korean American parents relied on faced many problems, among them limited institutional resources such as teachers and counselors who could adequately address the needs of the predominantly poor and minority and immigrant population they served. In addition, on occasion school counselors referred parents to Korean community-based programs that helped compensate for the schools' shortcomings with bilingual assistance; by and large, though, these resources were not widely available, were unknown to school staffs, and suffered from limited funding. Finally, when the Korean parents transferred their children from one public school to another, they were unable to escape the poverty, violence, and isolation endemic to these urban schools, and with each additional school, the students were less likely to put down roots and develop trusting and meaningful relationships. Consequently, they continued to navigate schooling alone and isolated and to grow increasingly alienated from the schooling process.

Neighborhood Public Schools

The working-class Korean parents were more likely to entrust the public schools with taking care of their children's education. Yet these schools, located in isolated communities serving predominantly poor minorities and immigrants, were faced with inadequate institutional resources and funding to meet the needs of the Korean parents and their children. They failed to provide the necessary bilingual assistance and accurate information regarding their children's schooling options, including a clear explanation of the difference between graduating with a high school diploma versus a GED.

Moreover, throughout the interviews, the Korean American dropouts explained how their educational experiences were marked by mistrust and poor relationships with teachers and school counselors. As I will illustrate in the following section, the students' schooling experience showed an overwhelming lack of mutual trust and respect between them and their teachers. Students consistently cited the lack of academic rigor, low expectations, and limited academic and social support in school as some of the reasons for dropping out. At the same time, their parents lacked the economic and social resources necessary to compensate for these institutional shortcomings. Their limited English skills, knowledge of the U.S. educational system, and time to devote to their children's schooling only added to the problem.

For instance, students explained that their parents rarely came to parent–teacher conferences although they often did meet with their children's school counselors after receiving numerous phone calls and letters—usually without Korean translation—from school. Moreover, students explained that when their parents came during school hours, it often meant that they would have to miss a day of work without pay, so some students tried to "take care" of the situation on their own without getting their parents involved. Sometimes this meant resorting to intercepting school mail and phone calls for their parents. However, according to Jay, even if parents went to the high school to meet with the school counselor, these meetings were often a "waste of time" and rarely helpful:

> It's a waste of time. My mom sits there with me as the counselor rattles things off to me in English so I can translate for my mom. I know I messed up, too, and could've done better, but it's not always my fault that kids can't learn in that school. The counselor thought that I'd be better off taking the GED, since my records were so bad . . . my mom eventually agreed and signed the papers.

Jay's comment illustrates the disadvantages faced by many low-income immigrant parents when they turn to their children's school for guidance. Without adequate English skills and knowledge of the U.S. education system, the working-class Korean American parents were often at the mercy of the schools themselves. Without adequate translation, the parents lacked accurate information and were unable to ask school personnel important questions regarding their children's schooling, legal rights, and other program references—information that is pivotal for making sound decisions about their children's schooling.

According to Mike, the director of the GED program at YCC, lack of bilingual counselors and translators is one of the biggest barriers facing Korean and other immigrant parents in New York City urban schools:

> I think many of them make some kind of effort to go to the school. Or they are forced to go because they have to sign papers or they are called in by the vice principal. And then they struggle through some sort of conversation, and basically they are directed by the guidance counselor basically saying that "your child is not doing well enough, or they are skipping too much and it would be better for your child to get their GED" is what basically comes out of the conversation in most cases. They go there, and some guidance counselors might tell the parents there are some programs they can go to, and some will just tell them to leave. I will either get calls from counselors . . . I get it from all different sides, students, guidance counselor, and the parents.

When I asked how New York City schools had been dealing with such limited bilingual assistance for parents, Theresa, another program administrator at YCC, explained that despite parents' legal rights and the educational policy mandated by the board of education, it was difficult to enforce such policy at the school level because of limited funds and resources. Theresa recalled a conversation she had had with one of the high school counselors:

> There aren't any translators and even though legally they [Korean parents] should be provided translators, when you mention that, they [counselors] just scoff at you, "What, are you joking?" Even people at the board of the education level will tell you this. But if you repeat it to a counselor at a high school, "I've never heard of this. Is that a joke?" I would tell them, "The board of ed told me," and they would say, "Well, that is obviously not going to happen."

Theresa continued to explain that the language barrier faced by Korean parents leads some of them to sign legal papers that release their children from school prematurely—a process that many Korean parents are not even aware of until they try to reenroll their children in school:

> One thing about the counselor issue, the language barrier, is that a lot of times the counselor will tell the parents to sign papers, and sometimes that's the very paper that says they are allowing their student to drop out of school. And the parent doesn't even know what they are signing. There have been numerous cases of that happening.

Mike agreed with Theresa and also commented on how the language barrier prohibits the Korean American parents from asking important questions and gaining information that could potentially help their children and keep them in school:

> And they can't ask appropriate questions because of the language barrier. What does it really mean to get a GED? Or how does this whole process take place? Are there any other options?

These are important questions that need to be addressed not only for Korean American parents but also for the growing number of immigrant parents who may find themselves in a similar predicament. The above scenarios illustrate how low-SES immigrant parents have little input in public schools, where they are often marginalized by administrators, teachers, and the schooling process itself (Fine, 1991; Noguera, 2003). In her study of high school dropouts in New York City, Fine (1991) documented the significant hurdles that urban schools face in providing their students and parents with adequate schooling resources. Anyon (1997) also referred to the political economy and larger structural forces at play, noting that the failure of urban schools can be attributed to the economic and social isolation of the communities in which they are situated. As Noguera (2003) has argued, however, public schools are becoming ever more critical sites for building and implementing institutional reform, precisely because they serve as one of the most reliable sources of social support for children. Especially for poor minorities and children of immigrants, urban public schools continue to be one of the few stable mainstream institutions to which they have access and a place that has the potential for providing equal opportunities (Noguera, 2003).

Transferring Students from One School to Another

One of the effects of poverty is that parents have to change residence depending on available jobs. For children, moving from one city to another also means changing schools. Not surprisingly, the Korean American high school dropouts in my study were more likely than the MH students to have moved to a different state and city and transferred schools, further inhibiting their ability to maintain strong ties to co-ethnic networks and to accumulate social capital in their respective schools and communities.

As an infant, Jane emigrated from Korea to the United States with her family. They moved frequently after arriving, mostly due to financial and housing constraints. She explained:

> When I moved from Korea to New York, every 2 years of my life I moved to another house. When I was a little baby, I lived in a studio in Brooklyn. We lived there because it was easy to find jobs for my dad. Two years after, my mom had my little sister. The house was too small, so we moved to Elmhurst . . . after living there for 2 years, we moved to Forest Hills. We had to move out again because they kicked us out of the house, due to too many kids.

Jane said that as she neared age 14, "I didn't get accepted to any high schools I wanted to attend, and my zoned school was not that good." So her parents moved yet again, this time so she could attend a better school. According to Jane, there were many students residing in urban neighborhoods with poor-quality schools, and most were not fortunate enough to get into an academic magnet high school. Consequently, their parents have to contend with moving from one school district to another in order to provide the best public education possible for their children.

For some of my informants, searching for a better-quality public school meant living apart from parents and moving in with relatives. For instance, Adam originally resided with his single mom in a Bronx housing project and went to his zoned public high school. But as he put it, "The school was in bad shape, and I got into fights all the time." So his mom sent him to live with his aunt in Queens so that he could transfer to another public high school. Meanwhile, she continued to live and work in the Bronx. Adam remarked, "I tried there, too, but soon, there was nothing holding me there, you know. I started to cut classes and hang out with friends."

Although the new high school in Queens had a better reputation than his old high school, it was nevertheless overcrowded; was populated mostly by poor, minority students; and had inadequate schooling resources. Moreover, given Adam's separation from his mother, her long working hours, and the limited parental supervision he received, he began to cut school, then stopped going altogether and eventually dropped out. As I will explain further in the next section, this parental strategy of moving children from one school to another with similar structural problems only increased the students' mobility rate, which in turn limited their access to social capital, increased their alienation from school, and further perpetuated the likelihood of their dropping out of high school.

LONG-TERM INVESTMENT IN EDUCATION VERSUS SHORT-TERM INCOME FROM WORK: REPRODUCTION OF SOCIAL AND ECONOMIC INEQUALITY

As illustrated, the YCC Korean parents, compared to the MH parents, faced myriad institutional barriers in gaining access to social capital and providing schooling support for their children. The findings in this research answer some important questions regarding class variance and social mobility within Korean American communities that have yet to be critically examined: If middle-class second-generation Korean Americans are more likely to leave their immigrant parental ethnic economy, does this pattern of economic mobility also hold true for working-class second-generation Korean Americans? What economic opportunities are available for working-class second-generation

Korean American children whose parents are not entrepreneurs, but instead work for other Korean business owners? How do Korean immigrant parents, in different social and economic contexts, adopt strategies to educate their children? And how does this process affect their children's investment and academic performance in schools?

Unlike the MH students, who were economically and socially supported by their parents to pursue education as a long-term investment that might eventually lead to opportunities outside the ethnic economy, the poor high school dropouts received limited economic and social support from their parents and communities to do so. Instead, given their low-income status, most of the high school dropouts had to earn a living and often had to choose between school and work. Therefore, in contrast to the MH students, who used education as a long-term investment to pursue career opportunities outside of their parents' ethnic economy, many of the high school dropouts followed in their parents' footsteps by working in menial positions for Korean entrepreneurs.

If the MH students studied at a private *hagwon* after school in order to gain entrance to a competitive college, the dropouts worked after school in order to contribute to their family income. When I asked Korean American high school dropouts whether their parents sent them to *hagwon* to help them with schoolwork, their response indicated that their family's low SES hindered their ability to attend. One student commented, "I went once or twice when I started high school, but my mom couldn't afford it. I also have to work after school, so who has the time?" His comment was typical of many of the dropouts I interviewed, many of whom had to work after school and believed that working for a salary, rather than paying to study, would be a better use of time given their low socioeconomic status. However, without a high school diploma, the dropouts were limited to low-status menial jobs in ethnic enclaves and were more likely to reproduce their immigrant parents' status in the ethnic economy.

According to the Korean American high school dropouts, because their positions were menial service jobs—working mostly for Korean entrepreneurs as manicurists, cashiers, valet parking attendants, nightclub bouncers, and the like—they were able to find work with relative ease. They described how employment with large corporate chains was harder to come by and how bilingual skills—more than a high school or other education credential—helped them find work with Korean entrepreneurs, since these business owners often serviced an English-speaking clientele. Finally, although the dropouts admitted that they did not necessarily "learn anything" at their menial jobs, they stressed that they nevertheless "got paid." As Amy explained:

> After I dropped out, I stayed home and started working at a nail salon and worked as a receptionist in office. The nail salon was

> through my mom. They want someone who can speak English for office work. You don't learn anything, you just get paid. I worked in the Korean community 'cause it's a lot harder to work for Gap or Banana Republic. It's a lot easier to get jobs in the Korean community.

Thus, the advantages of working in Korean ethnic enclaves were not lost on the dropouts. The ethnic economy provided them with a chance to financially support their family and themselves while in school, or it afforded them an opportunity to continue working even without a high school diploma, after dropping out. Although they understood that a college degree would give them more opportunities, they also explained that they might not necessarily need it to "make a living." That is, for some of the Korean American high school dropouts, the initial ease of obtaining work in the Korean ethnic economy also falsely misled them to believe that they might not necessarily need a high school diploma.

> I think even without a high school diploma, you can always get jobs. Maybe not as much as college degree, but you can always get office jobs everywhere. I think that my friends don't believe that you need education to make a living. The girls work in a nail salon, and the guys work in stores, restaurants, or sell cell phones.

Other studies of high school dropouts also show that although work may be seen as an important means of adolescent socialization, it may also perpetuate students' disengagement with schooling, depending on the kinds of jobs and the reasons for employment (McNeal, 1997; Rumberger & Larson, 1998)

However, for the older high school dropouts who had been in the workforce for a few years, the reality of trying to earn a living without a college degree, let alone a high school diploma, hit home. Such experiences convinced these kids to take the GED and go back to school. For instance, Ken had dropped out of high school several years earlier. He found work in a small startup Korean technology company without a high school diploma but quickly learned that he could not climb the company ladder or earn a salary comparable to those of college graduates. When the Korean company folded, he attended a technical college and tried to obtain jobs in "American" companies. He learned that most of these companies required at least a college degree even to get an interview. Consequently, he decided to earn a GED so that he could attend college. As he explained:

> I used to do computer work and used to work for a Korean. But because I don't have a high school diploma, they paid me lower than others, and because my English was bad, they would give the job to someone else. So, you can get a job in the Korean company, but

> without a high school diploma, they pay you less. When I wanted to apply to an American company, I couldn't even get in the door because the minimum requirement is a college diploma.

Like Ken, other Korean students who experienced such occupational barriers tried to go back to school, pass the GED, and apply to vocational schools, community colleges, and city and state universities. Certainly, the availability of menial jobs in the ethnic economy provided the dropouts with important source of economic resources that served as a potential stepping stone to obtain higher education and social mobility. However, as the director of the GED program at YCC explained, this path is neither guaranteed nor obvious. "Some students drop out of high school, work for a while, then realize they can't make enough to earn a living or need a college degree to get ahead. So, they come back to take their GED. Although some students pass their exam and go on to college, others never come back to the GED program after the first few sessions."

However, during their high school years, Korean American high school dropouts are less likely to see the direct link between schooling and economic mobility, and they doubt that schooling is a worthwhile financial investment that will "pay off." To the contrary, most of the dropouts had to rely on short-term work to get by, forced to choose between earning a living or continuing in school.

To summarize, although both groups of Korean American parents similarly valued education, they used different educational strategies in their children's schooling. My findings indicate that the MH Korean parents had an easier time than the Korean parents of dropouts when it came to supporting their children in using education as a long-term investment. For the MH parents, this meant enabling their children to leave the ethnic economy for opportunities in the mainstream economy. To reach this goal, the parents turned to their co-ethnic immigrant networks and adopted parental strategies such as hiring private tutors and counselors and sending their children to tuition-based after-school academies. Embedded in strong networks such as those found in co-ethnic churches and equipped with socioeconomic resources and college degrees, the middle-class parents were able to intervene in their children's education and provide them with important schooling resources, including bilingual support that was not readily available at the school.

The Korean parents of dropouts adopted different educational strategies premised on their limited economic and social resources. Most worked long hours, and many were single mothers, both of which made it difficult to provide adequate supervision at home or to intervene effectively, if at all, in their children's education. Unable to afford private, tuition-based schools and private tutors, the working-class parents were forced to rely solely on neighborhood public schools to provide schooling for their children. However, located in poor neighborhoods and populated mainly by poor, minority students, these schools were resource-strained and incapable of providing adequate support for either the children or the parents. Moreover, given their low socioeconomic status, many of the high school dropouts had to take after-school jobs, mostly as menial workers in the ethnic economy, where many continued in these jobs after dropping out. That is, the MH Korean students were more likely to use education as a means to leave the ethnic economy, compared to the low-income Korean high school dropouts, who continued to work in the ethnic economy as menial workers, thereby reproducing the economic status of their low-status immigrant parents. Students' comments poignantly illustrate how co-ethnic networks may be both beneficial as well as limited, depending on changing contexts. The myriad structural barriers experienced by low-income parents, combined with their children's own daily experience within their limited opportunity structure and inadequate schools, led many of the dropouts to resist education as a viable long-term investment. Their comments poignantly illustrate how their decision to drop out of high school was also a form of adaptation and resistance to the limited social and economic opportunities available to them (MacLeod, 1995; Willis, 1977).

PART II

Gaining Schooling Resources and Institutional Support: Peer Networks, Social Capital, and Identities

As illustrated in Part I, strong ties to first-generation parents and co-ethnic networks provide important economic and social resources for Korean American students. However, children of Asian immigrants are not raised exclusively within the confines of their nuclear families and co-ethnic networks. They are raised and socialized in a variety of social networks—including schools—that represent disparate social spheres with different sets of cultural codes and social actors (Boykin, 1986; Boykin & Toms, 1985; Gee, 1989; Phelan, Davidson, & Yu, 1993). How they gain and accumulate important resources in mainstream institutions such as schools depends not only on a variety of socioeconomic factors but also on their ability to cross and bridge these disparate networks and discourses (Stanton-Salazar, 1997, 2001). Both the economic opportunities afforded by their families and communities, and the institutional characteristics of schools themselves, play a major role in facilitating or hampering students' cross-cultural acculturation.

Regarding the schools, scholars have identified instrumental ties and access to supportive teachers and counselors as valuable for children's academic success and occupational mobility (Croninger & Lee, 2001; De Graaf & Flap, 1988; Stanton-Salazar, 2001; Valenzuela, 1999). However, low-income students living and attending schools in poor neighborhoods are at a disadvantage compared to their middle-class counterparts in gaining access to and building relationships with such institutional agents (Stanton-Salazar, 1997, 2001). Many low-income minority students are literally cut off from the capital, social networks, and institutional gatekeepers needed to gain jobs, college guidance, and career opportunities for economic mobility (Anyon, 1997; Fine, 1991; Wehlage & Rutter, 1986).

Therefore, it is important to examine how institutional characteristics of schools may either inhibit or promote access to important gatekeepers and other schooling resources. In doing so, educators can identify various obstacles to accumulating social capital faced by poor communities, and they can also identify structural factors and key institutional actors critical to building social capital (Saegert et al., 2001). Such an examination of the obstacles poor communities face reveals that the process of accumulating social capital is far from neutral (Bernstein, 1975; Bourdieu & Passeron, 1977; Lareau, 2003; Stanton-Salazar, 2001).

By comparing the experiences of Korean American students in two very different schooling contexts, this part illustrates how academic achievement greatly depends on the institutional characteristics of the school—that is, its ability to foster trusting and caring relations between students and key gatekeepers, such as teachers and counselors, and to reinforce the accumulation of social capital among students and parents by providing adequate schooling resources and college guidance for all students.

Although both groups of Korean American students in this study attended New York City public high schools, the institutional characteristics and cultures of the two schools could not have been more different. By passing a competitive entrance exam, the students at MH were admitted to one of the most academically rigorous high schools in the city, one rooted in a highly academic culture and a college-bound curriculum and populated mostly by middle-class Asian American and White students. In this context, the Korean American students received not only exemplary training but also important schooling resources, including at least some support and guidance from teachers and counselors. To some extent, these key gatekeepers helped the Korean American students cross institutional borders between their home and school as well as accumulate educational resources needed for achieving in school.

By contrast, the Korean American high school dropouts attended urban high schools in poor neighborhood, schools that were populated predominantly by poor, minority, and immigrant children and that were poorly funded, overcrowded, and marked by high levels of school violence and daunting dropout rates. In order to avoid these schools, as well as their own poor school records, the dropouts resorted to transferring from one school to another, resulting in a high mobility rate that only alienated them further from schooling. Faced with scarce support from teachers and counselors in schools and lacking access to strong social capital at home and in their communities, these students adopted behaviors at odds with academic achievement, disengaging from school through absenteeism, cutting classes, fighting, and suspension, which further increased their likelihood of dropping out. Unlike the MH students, who had at least some support from teachers and counselors, the Korean American high school dropouts consistently referred to being isolated and alone, navigating through the education system without much adult guidance.

Equally notable is that because of their widely disparate schooling contexts, as well as the different social and economic resources embedded in their kinship and peer networks, the two groups of students adopted very different educational strategies and very different peer network orientations—and achieved very different results. In both cases, the Korean American students themselves built peer networks that played an integral role in helping them obtain what they needed. As active agents, rather than mere passive recipients, both groups of students learned to adapt, negotiate, and resist their immigrant parents' values and expectations, in effect constructing their own peer networks to acquire resources or to address issues specific to them. These included locating concrete schooling, college, or job and career guidance; grappling with intergenerational conflicts; and negotiating their racial and ethnic identities.

By now, it should be no surprise that the MH students found it much easier than the dropouts to access key gatekeepers who were willing and able to provide guidance with schooling, the college application process, and career opportunities. Less obvious is that the MH students relied on their peer networks in school to increase both the pool of institutional agents from which they could draw and their access to them. Because the gatekeepers and the information they offered were of higher status, the MH students were able to use these youth-based networks not only to compensate for the limitations of their immigrant parents but also to *advance* their own educational and career opportunities.

The Korean American dropouts, on the other hand, built kinship and peer networks predominantly comprised of other low-income high school dropouts who were employed in the ethnic economy or had joined the military. Although they gained information that was important to them—about menial service jobs in ethnic economy, joining the military, and publicly funded GED programs—that information held lower value in, and was rewarded less by, the mainstream economy. Therefore, compared to the Korean American students at MH, the high school dropouts were more likely to use their peer networks to *overcome* institutional obstacles.

What should not be lost in these findings is that both groups of Korean American students faced racial discrimination and marginalization. How they negotiated their racial and ethnic identities also was dictated, in no small part, by their different school contexts and peer relations. Equipped with strong social capital at home and at school, the MH students developed resilience in dealing with stratifying forces such as racism. Considered perpetual foreigners despite having been born or raised in the United States, they firmly believed that working harder in school was imperative to gaining opportunities in society. That is, they used education as a strategy to compensate, in part, for the stigma that accompanied their racial minority status.

By contrast, given the limited social and economic support they received at home and at school, as well as their living in isolated urban neighborhoods, the dropouts were more vulnerable to stratifying forces such as poverty and racism. They were also more apt to adopt an oppositional cultural frame of reference as a way to resist this racial and economic inequality. In effect, they aligned their experiences with those of other poor racial minorities—Blacks, Hispanics, and other Asians—while at the same time distinguishing themselves from "wealthy" and "educated" Korean and other Asian Americans, whose attributes of "success" they associated with Whiteness. That is, in the context of the model minority stereotype that often conflates Asians with Whiteness, the low-status Korean American high school dropouts negotiated their identities differently from other racial minorities, underscoring the integral relationship between race and class.

This part highlights the significance of race and class, as well as schooling context, in accounting for academic achievement among Asian American children. It also illustrates how the co-ethnic economy and networks may be both beneficial and limited, noting the significance of access to institutional resources in and outside of co-ethnic networks to the success of second-generation children in school. Thus it demonstrates how students' success *and* failure are integrally based on structural resources available at home, in the community, and at school, and how students themselves negotiate and resist the larger stratifying forces of poverty and racism.

CHAPTER 4

Magnet High's Korean American Students: Advancing Educational Opportunities

> I learn most of things from my Korean friends. I hang out with more studious people, so our topics are about college, tests, grades, and stuff like that. I have this one friend who is really smart, and she is always doing better, and then I would just be, like, "Ugh, I am slacking off, and she is doing so much better." And it motivates me that way. There isn't an intense competition, but you know when your friends are doing better, and it's not like you hate them for it, but you feel a slight twinge of jealousy and, "Wow, I wish I can get her grades." You know, I ask about what classes I should be taking, colleges, and stuff like what would be good for extracurricular activities. You just learn this from friends.
>
> —Sun Myung, age 17

ACADEMIC HIGH SCHOOL CONTEXT: (RE)CONSTRUCTING SECOND-GENERATION PEER NETWORKS

When I met Sun Myung, she was a junior at MH preparing to apply for colleges. She was late for our interview, coming from lunch with her friends at the cafeteria, where they had been deeply engrossed in a conversation about colleges, test scores, and the GPAs they needed to get into the colleges of their choice. Taking a deep breath, she sat down and confided in me how stressful the college application process was for her and her friends. Despite the difficulty of the process, however, she explained that her friends helped and supported one another. While Sun Myung and other Korean American students at MH gained important schooling information from teachers and counselors, their main source was Korean and other Asian American peers at school, who themselves often learned about the college application process from their kinship, community, and school ties. As explained above, Sun Myung's friends, in addition to motivating her to compete and excel in school, also provided concrete information on schooling and colleges.

At MH, one of the most competitive elite public high schools in New York City, the students were steeped in a competitive college-bound curriculum taught by teachers who are certified in their fields. Students were also surrounded predominantly by middle-class White and Asian American peers who were immersed in this school culture that fostered academic achievement and excellence; thus, the Korean American students at MH were likely to associate with peers of similar socioeconomic status, education background, and academic expectations. Even for those Korean American students at MH whose families were of lower socioeconomic status were more likely to be exposed to and to associate with other students of higher socioeconomic backgrounds. Moreover, by attending a high school where second-generation Asian Americans represented nearly half (46.5% percent) of the student population, the Korean American students were likely to reinforce old or establish new friendships with other Asian and Korean American peers who also shared similar experiences growing up as children of immigrant parents. In this respect, institutional characteristics of the school played an important role in strengthening peer relations and helping second-generation youths achieve academically.

Students admitted that prior to coming to MH, they did not have a history of attending schools with such a large number of Asian Americans. While some students had attended neighborhood elementary and middle schools consisting predominantly of middle-class White students, others had attended schools consisting mostly of poor Blacks and Hispanics. As mentioned earlier, however, many of the Korean American students at MH had established ties to other Korean Americans prior to entering high school—through church, *hagwon*, tae kwon do, or other community organizations. Since, for most of my informants, being in a school with such a large Asian American population was a relatively new phenomenon, they had an increased likelihood of reinforcing, or even expanding, their circle of Asian American friends on arriving to MH. Furthermore, school now became an important mainstream institution where children of immigrants could come together and further exchange important information regarding schooling, colleges, and career opportunities.

Kevin, a junior at MH, explained how his mostly second-generation Korean American friends maintained a relatively close social network through contacts at school, in community organizations, and in churches. He noted that it was typical for Korean American youths to know each other from various social settings, referring to his network as "one big circle":

> The Korean community of my age group, everyone knows everyone in some way. Like, either you're friends with someone that knows this other person . . . it's like everything is sort of related into one big circle, if you know what I mean. Since I started out with Korean

> friends and they got to know more Korean friends and then whenever, I started hanging out with them, and then more other Korean friends . . . church especially, tae kwon do, neighborhood, they are, like, all causes.

According to the students I interviewed, this regular contact with Korean Americans in myriad settings formed the basis for an important set of shared experiences; namely, those derived from growing up as second-generation children with immigrant parents. Connie remarked that her friends, most of whom were Korean and other Asian American, also operated under an "indirect set of rules" that they adhered to as a result of growing up with immigrant parents. According to Connie, such rules and expectations brought her and other Asian American friends closer together, at the same time setting them apart from some of her Caucasian friends:

> Most of my friends are Korean. I met a few of them here [in school] and a few close friends at church. I've been at the church for nearly 5 to 6 years. I can relate to them 'cause Korean culture has a lot of indirect set of rules. There is a certain amount of respect that you have to give to elders. Just the way you obey your parents . . . even the way you talk to your elders is different from the way Caucasians talk to their parents. I guess there is a lot of strictness with them. It's easier to relate to Koreans or Asians as friends than other races. My friends, from what they tell me, it seems to me similar between Koreans and Chinese and other Asians. The standard of how they want their child to do is the same. I know my parents are really demanding. A lot of my Asian friends also have demanding parents.

As with the students in this study, other studies have also indicated that second-generation Korean and Chinese college students increased their circle of ethnic and pan-ethnic friends because of shared experiences and expectations growing up as children of Asian immigrants (Kibria, 2002; Louie, 2004). And research on peer relations has also pointed out that students are more likely to form friendships with those who have similar backgrounds, goals, and values and who are perceived as being trustworthy (Hallinan & Sorensen, 1985; Hallinan & Williams, 1990; Stanton-Salazar & Spina, 2005).

However, if sharing similar parental expectations was one reason for associating with other second-generation Korean and other Asian American peers, another compelling reason was the shared limitations of their immigrant parents. As noted in the previous section, because of their limited English skills and knowledge of the U.S. education system, most MH parents could not be relied on to directly provide schooling or homework assistance to their children or personally to advise them on the college application process. And while they compensated for this with their higher socioeconomic status, educational backgrounds, and social capital in their respective ethnic communities, which gave them an advantage over the working-class parents of Korean American high school dropouts, they were nevertheless at a disadvantage compared to native-born, White, middle-class parents.

Unlike children from middle-class White families, whose social network is already integrally connected to mainstream institutional resources, minority children from immigrant families have to negotiate the boundaries of their own family and ethnic communities in order to access gatekeepers in mainstream institutions such as schools. While most White middle-class students could readily rely on their parents to act as institutional gatekeepers and help them navigate school and the college application process, most of the Korean American students at MH had to rely on individuals other than their parents for schooling, college, and career guidance. That is, while White middle-class parents act as institutional agents themselves, or engage with institutional agents as status equals or even status superiors, low-income minority and immigrant parents are more likely to operate from a subordinate position, dependent on institutional gatekeepers to provide schooling resources and support for their children (Stanton-Salazar, 1997, 2001).

Like so many Korean American students at MH, Paul explained that although his parents had high academic expectations of him, their ability to help him directly was hampered by their limited knowledge of how the school and college system works in the United States. So, rather than turning to his parents for schooling guidance, he resorted to his friends in school. In fact, as far back as middle school he had learned about the specialized magnet high schools through his friends. In high school he continued to rely on his Korean American peers as the main source of schooling support. He reiterated sentiments expressed by other Korean American students, who confessed that although their parents harbored high expectations and provided economic support, they were rarely in a position to directly provide useful guidance on schooling and colleges. As a result, Paul rarely turned to his parents regarding schooling. Instead, he relied mostly on his friends.

> I heard about specialized high schools in seventh grade . . . junior high school didn't tell me anything about it . . . they didn't really motivate the kids to take it. Through my Korean friends, I heard about it. I get most of my information now from friends. Friends would ask each other how they are doing in school, and we would find out how to sign up for SATs. If I need help, I would seek them. I don't go to my parents because they seem single-minded. They want me to get 1,400 on SAT get into Harvard, Yale, Princeton. The first three words they learn when they come to America are *Harvard*,

> *Yale*, *Princeton*. So I don't really ask them for any information. If I need books, they would surely buy [them] for me. They would support me financially . . . that's pretty much it.

These parental limitations became even more evident when Korean American students needed to obtain internships and other career opportunities outside of the ethnic economy. For instance, Mia was an 18-year-old senior who immigrated to the United States at age 6. She contrasted her Asian American friends' lack of access to mainstream institutions with the myriad opportunities her Caucasian friends had. She recommended that Korean American parents teach their children to develop institutional discourses, or "social skills," so that they learn how to communicate across economic and social boundaries:

> I see a lot of my Caucasian friends who have all these opportunities 'cause their parents know people from a company, and they get a job there as an intern. And a lot of Asians lack those kind of connections, I guess. Because all we ever do is grocery stores, nail salons, I think parents should support them more and let them get social skills earlier. I see 15- to 16-year-olds that can't communicate with others. They are in silence . . . [a] lot of young Korean students lack social skills. I think the parents should support them to have a regular social teenage life with internships and stuff, because they don't have parental support.

Mia's poignant response highlighted the disadvantages of growing up with immigrant parents who are limited in their English-language proficiency, knowledge of the U.S. education system, and access to resources in the mainstream economy. She was keenly aware that growing up as a child of an immigrant family meant having limited access and connections to institutional resources that could help socialize and prepare her for a mainstream job and career opportunities.

Consequently, she turned to her peers, who through their combined networks pooled schooling information and provided access to gatekeepers and institutional agents. These youth-based networks at school, or what I refer to as a "second-generation peer networks," formed the basis of the MH students' institutional knowledge. Embedded within these networks were important gatekeepers such as teachers and counselors at their public high school, private tutors and counselors, and teachers from after-school academies in Korean ethnic enclaves. However, the greatest number of gatekeepers within their youth-based networks consisted of older second-generation friends and mentors who had gone through the U.S. education system or had experience working in the mainstream economy. Among these were siblings and cousins, older classmates or alumni from school, and family friends and adults from church and neighborhood.

This form of bilingual and bicultural support was significant precisely because it could help the Korean American students cross disparate social and linguistic boundaries between home and school. For instance, research on Hispanic students shows that those who are bilingual and have a bicultural network have special advantages over their monolingual English-speaking and Spanish-speaking counterparts in acquiring institutional support (Stanton-Salazar & Dornbusch, 1995; Suárez-Orozco & Suárez-Orozco, 1995, 2001). English-language skills gave bilingual students the cultural capital needed to access educational resources in mainstream institutions, while the Spanish-language skills helped them maintain close ties to first-generation parents and communities who protected them from succumbing to the stratifying forces of poverty and racism and from adopting the oppositional cultural frame of reference so prevalent among those in poor urban communities. In other words, they learned to develop resilience and cultivate support by remaining embedded in familial and communal support systems, while learning how to cross mainstream institutional borders to gain access to key institutional actors—those individuals who have the capacity and commitment to provide directly, or negotiate the transmission of, schooling resources and career opportunities (Stanton-Salazar, 1997, 2001).

The significance of kinship ties and familial support are historically rooted in minority families who are marginalized from mainstream institutional resources (Stack, 1974; Saegert et al., 2001). Ties to both kin and ethnic networks ("strong" ties), as well as to institutional actors outside immediate kinship networks ("weak" ties), are important for building social capital (Granovetter, 1985). In the case of Korean Americans at MH, their second-generation peer networks increased their likelihood of accessing both strong and weak ties, while reinforcing the bicultural network that proves so helpful for children of immigrants. It is also important to note that the MH students had an advantage over Korean American high school dropouts in accumulating social capital because individuals in their networks came from higher socioeconomic and educational backgrounds—an important factor that increases their likelihood of gaining access to resources of more value in mainstream institutions such as school.

Furthermore, the findings illustrated that the children of immigrants were not mere passive recipients who adopted parental messages wholesale: Instead, as active agents they adapted, negotiated, and resisted parental messages and expectations. By constructing their own second-generation peer networks, the Korean American students at MH learned to gain important institutional and emotional support that addressed experiences and satisfied needs specific to them—anything from schooling information and college guidance to conflict with parents to negotiation of race and ethnic identities (Lew, 2003b).

ACCESSING SCHOOLING AND INSTITUTIONAL RESOURCES THROUGH SECOND-GENERATION PEER NETWORKS

Teachers and Counselors

During their junior year at MH, every student was assigned a college adviser who evaluated the students' academic record, helped them choose appropriate colleges to apply to based on their GPA and standardized test scores, and helped them through the college application process. Some of my informants met with and sought help from their college counselors, while others sought help from their teachers at MH. Tom, a senior preparing to graduate, did both. Throughout his high school years, he resorted to his history teacher, Mr. Smith, and his guidance counselor for academic guidance and did so again during his college application process. When I met him in the spring semester of his senior year, Tom was thrilled to have just received an acceptance letter from the college of his choice. He was planning to study engineering there, with a minor in architecture, and was grateful for the guidance and advice he had received from his teacher and counselor. He indicated that his parents had never heard of the college but were pleased that he had applied there and was now planning to study engineering. Furthermore, given his family's financial constraints, he was thrilled that his parents would not have to pay for his college tuition:

> She [my counselor] thought that I could get in and encouraged me to apply early. It took a while to convince my parents, since they never heard of the school. But now, they are really happy that I got in . . . the free tuition helps a lot. Before applying there, I asked Mr. Smith, and he thought I would be pretty happy there. I wanted to stay near New York, you know. He has always been really helpful. He cares about his students and is willing to help us out. Many of us go to him, since he's been doing this for a long time here. I learned a lot in his class, and he helped me with school and recommendations for college.

Tom went on to say that as a senior getting ready to graduate, he advised his friend Phillip, a junior at MH whom Tom knew from their Korean church in Bayside, Queens, to seek a school counselor for advice on applying to college; he referred him to Mr. Smith. Tom explained, "Phillip is a junior now and getting ready to apply to college. I know how hard it was to go through that process, so I try to help him out and give him some tips, you know. I also told him to get help from his college adviser and Mr. Smith, since they know a lot more about this stuff."

Throughout my interviews, Korean American students at MH spoke not only of helping one another directly but also of mentioning adults who could provide assistance. Many also spoke of giving and receiving referrals to private tutors and college counselors in Korean ethnic enclaves—older second-generation Korean Americans with experience in and knowledge of the U.S. education and college system. As mentioned earlier, some Korean students preferred these private tutors and counselors to public school counselors because of the individual attention they offered as well as their bilingual skills, which enabled students to include their monolingual parents in their college application process. As Korean American parents at MH learned about tutors and counselors through their friends and hired them for their children's schooling, their children also learned about tutors and counselors through their peers in school, church, and community organizations, creating an ever-expanding pool for them to draw on and refer others to.

For instance, Susan commented that her friend had referred her to a Korean American teacher at *hagwon*. She noted that because the teacher had been born in the United States and had graduated from U.C. Berkeley, he was able to provide important schooling information and college guidance. Her comments indicated how grateful she was to have found him during her sophomore year, when she needed to prepare for college exams:

> I don't turn to my parents because they really don't know much about universities. I used to go to this after-school program in Queens, and the [Korean] teacher who still teaches there used to give me all this advice about colleges and universities and stuff. He went to Berkeley, and he knows what it's like to have a college life here and stuff. I talked to him, and he gave me good advice . . . like my first year, I didn't know that my grade was going into my transcript. I didn't even know what a transcript was. And then I messed up. In my freshman year, I failed a class and had to go to summer school, and I really didn't know the importance of studying until my sophomore year, 'cause that's when I got to know the teacher at the academy. He is the one who taught me about American colleges and universities and high schools. So that's when I really knew that I had to study, study, study.

Siblings, Older Mentors, and Peers

Besides resorting to teachers and counselors at the public high school and private academies in Korean ethnic enclaves, many students went to their older siblings for schooling guidance. Some students mentioned that because their older siblings were more knowledgeable about school processes and requirements, they often acted as a second set of parents. Luke fell into this category. Since one of his older brothers was a senior at New York University who understood the U.S. school system, he was often more strict with Luke than were his parents:

> I have four parents: my parents and two brothers. It's mostly my brothers who would look through my notes and say, "What are you doing in school? How come you never show me your test grades? Every time I ask how you are doing in school, you say you are doing good, but then how come you have a C?" If I fail, I am dead. Sometimes, I don't show my report card, but in a week I would show them, 'cause I don't want to get caught.

In the case of Kevin, it was his older sister who guided him in schooling and the college application process. He noted that she gave him important and concrete advice on exams, deadlines, and applications. He explained that unlike his parents, who stressed only academic grades and test scores, his sister advised him to be more involved in extracurricular activities in addition to doing well on college entrance exams. When I asked him whom he turned to for schooling and college guidance, he replied:

> Through my sister. She is 4 years ahead of me. Sometimes, she tries to help me out, but in actuality, she often passes down her views of what she wants me to do rather than what I want to do. My parents want me to go to a good college, but they think that grades and SATs are all that gets you in, when in actuality, it's a lot of extracurricular activities that you do.

In addition to turning to their siblings, the Korean American students at MH tapped older second-generation Korean American mentors and friends in their respective Korean churches. For instance, throughout most of her years at Magnet High, Kim relied on older Korean American mentors at her Korean church for school guidance. Recently, she had turned mostly to her friend Jennette, whose older brother was attending Columbia University. Through him, they both learned about college and career opportunities. Kim recounted her experience as a sophomore, when she had little knowledge about various college exams and applications—that is, until she received assistance from her Korean American friends and mentors:

> Most of the time, it's [college information] from older people in college that I met through friends. They told me what I should be doing. Like, I didn't know that I should be taking SAT II until sophomore year and that was from older people from my church who told me to take it.

Similarly, when I spoke to Harry, another junior at MH seeking schooling support from older Korean American peers, he remarked how older classmates and mentors, with their personal experiences and knowledge about standardized exams and the college application process, gave him concrete advice to plan ahead. "Like, the seniors who already applied to colleges, they tell me not to slack off junior year especially, and tell me to do certain things. And since I have a little more time than they do, they say that I should do better on achievements."

When asked, "Who do you turn to for information on colleges and schooling?" students consistently replied that they relied mostly on their Korean American peers at school and co-ethnic communities. That is, most of the Korean American students at MH used their youth-based networks to access key institutional agents who provided concrete schooling and college guidance. They also obtained concrete information directly from their peers. Song Hee explained that through a "big network," important schooling information was passed along from one friend to another:

> Usually [Korean] friends. I ask them questions and they know. They say, "Go over there and get those forms," or whatever. Specifically, I have one friend who is pretty active in school government and school community, so he is the one who I go to for information, 'cause he knows all the information and has access to all the forms and stuff. I get my information from friends. It's like a big network, where information is passed from one person to another . . . mostly through word of mouth.

The advantages of these social networks were readily apparent, but not all of the Korean American MH students participated and benefited from them. As a senior who had very little contact with Korean American communities, both in and outside of the school, Vicki explained how exclusive the Korean Americans could be at MH. She explained that while the Korean American students in the school "support and protect" one another, they could also act as "separatists." Her comments highlighted how social networks could also have negative attributes, perpetuating exclusion and segregation (Portes, 1988).

> The Korean groups here [school], on a positive note, are very interconnected and tight with each other . . . it's like a wolf-pack mentality. If someone messes with one, everyone knows about it, and they all support and protect each other. In the bad sense, they are very egocentric: "If you are not one of us, you can't join us." That really bothers me. I am not boastful about my race, and I don't think I should be judged by what I am but who I am. You shouldn't be exactly alike and conform. The group has too much structure, and I never wanted to be a part of it . . . very separatist.

When I asked Vicki how her parents influenced her perspective, she explained that her father, who was educated in the United States, believed that in order for her to succeed in society she had to "assimilate," and that by being bound to the Korean community, she might limit her ability to "succeed." Born and raised in Westchester County, north of New York City, and surrounded by predominantly White middle-class suburban families, Laura never learned to speak Korean. And because her parents had been educated in the United States and spoke fluent English, she turned to them for school guidance and career advice:

> My dad came here when he was very young to get a college degree, and he knows that in order to succeed, you have to assimilate. So, being too much involved with the Korean community may be bad. My parents know that there is a brain child in school with a perfect SAT score, but for my parents, they just want me to be a good kid—not just have good grades, but a whole person—and they give me all this freedom and options so that I am not forced into something. They present the options, and then it's up to me to choose . . . I want to study law because I've always been interested in speaking my part. It was presented to me by my parents, but it's ultimately up to me.

Unlike Vicki, however, most of the Korean American students in the study could not obtain schooling guidance directly from their immigrant parents. Compared to Vicki, the majority of Korean American students at MH were at a disadvantage in moving between home and a mainstream institution such as high school. As we have seen, such movement and adaptation across institutional borders often proves difficult. Most had to rely on someone other than their immigrant parents to access institutional agents and gatekeepers who could provide important schooling and college guidance.

By critically examining how Korean American students generate and maintain second-generation peer networks in and outside of school, the research revealed various structural and institutional barriers that many children of Asian immigrants must overcome to achieve academically. At a glance, it would be easy to assume that the students in this research were passive "model minority" Asian American students who were admitted to a competitive magnet high school, were academically successful, and ultimately achieved social mobility purely because of the values of education and the work ethic instilled by their first-generation parents and ethnic networks. However, this research explicates the ways in which, as active agents, students learned to reconstruct a second-generation youth-based network consisting of key institutional resources they needed to achieve academically. Their experiences illustrate the importance of peer networks and how the bilingual and bicultural orientation they foster helped the MH students gain structural resources from both their first- and second-generation communities. Far from being passive, the students negotiate a complex set of variables in order to move between ethnic enclaves and mainstream institutions.

Thus, minority students' ability to access institutional resources depended upon effective participation in what Delpit (1988) called the dominant "culture of power." At the same time, Korean American students at MH learned to engage in the academic process communally, rather than individually. That is, while they learned to cross institutional borders, they remained embedded in familial and communal support systems. The challenge of participating in the dominant "culture of power," then, entails learning the appropriate "codes" and gaining access to gatekeepers who can provide institutional schooling resources, while reinforcing one's own ethnic and cultural backgrounds (Boykin, 1986; Boykin & Toms, 1985; Gee, 1989; Neisser, 1986).

As Stanton-Salazar (1997) noted, "In sum, the development of social ties to institutional agents is crucial to the social development and empowerment of ethnic minority children and youth precisely because these ties represent consistent and reliable sources from which they can learn the appropriate decoding skills and from which they can obtain other key forms of institutional support" (p. 15). Therefore, social capital may be valuable insofar as a member in the community is connected to mainstream institutional agents and insofar as that individual is committed and able to provide the children with access to "funds of knowledge" that they need to navigate through mainstream institutions such as school (Stanton-Salazar, 2001).

As such, in order to bridge the gap between educational aspirations and achievement, the Korean American students at MH needed more than to internalize the value their parents placed on education. They needed concrete schooling support and key institutional actors who could provide them with structural resources for fulfilling their educational aspirations. That is, school achievement for all children, including Asian Americans, has to be placed in an institutional context, where success in school depends on access to structural resources, such as key gatekeepers, social capital, and concrete schooling support.

ROLE OF SECOND-GENERATION PEER NETWORKS IN NEGOTIATING PARENTAL EXPECTATIONS AND IDENTITIES

It is important to note that in addition to gaining schooling resources, the Korean American students also acquired important emotional and moral support through their youth networks—usually for issues specific to second-generation children such as managing conflict with immigrant parents, confronting racism, and negotiating racial and ethnic identities.

Mia, who was in the process of taking college exams, turned to her mostly Korean and Chinese American school friends for help in dealing with school pressures. She also looked to them for important emotional support when she had problems with her parents at home:

> I talk to my friends about colleges—a lot of colleges, SATs, and stuff. I am frustrated 'cause I don't know what to do with college application. It's hard. There's a lot to do, and you don't know how to start, so I talk to friends about the whole application thing. We also talk about parents. If you have problems with parents, we talk about family problems, fights with our parents. I find most of the Korean parents to be strict, and they can't really understand how American high school works, so we kind of have troubles. Because I don't think they really understand what it's like to be in American high school, so I personally get into fights a lot with them. So, I talk about it with my friends, and they are able to understand it better 'cause their parents are like that, too.

Students noted how conflicts with parents involve complex negotiation and how they struggle to achieve a delicate balance between respecting their parents' views and expressing their own opinions. Some students explained that their parents often equated being "American" with loss of respect for elders—that is, the opposite of what it means to be "Korean." Gina reiterated the term *chon dae mal*, a formal way of speaking to elders in Korean, to illustrate this point:

> You know how, in Korea, there are two ways of speaking, one to your friends and the other way to older people, like *chon dae mal*. My parents wouldn't let me use anything but *chon dae mal*. In America, there is no real set formal way to speak to older people. In America, it's being polite. In Korea, it's being more than polite; it's being respectful.

Gina explained that her parents refer to *chon dae mal* as an important sign of respecting her elders and maintaining ties to the Korean heritage and ethnicity. When she asserted her own voice and disagreed with her parents, it was often construed as talking back, and she was chastised of being too "Americanized." For Gina and others, such conflict with parents frequently forced them to polarize their bicultural experience—a process that was difficult and fraught with anger and frustration. Gina elaborated:

> So, in that way, my parents don't want me to be Americanized and cultural things and values and concepts. They get mad when I don't follow their ways . . . when I try to talk back to my parents, they really don't like it. They say, "Oh, there is that American teenagers." "Oh," they say, "that's not going to work in this house." I tried to express my opinion, but they see it as talking back. I say, "This is how I think."

Once conflicts had occurred and discipline had been meted out, tension between students and parents persisted. Janice explained that many Korean parents, including her own, had high academic expectations but often resorted to what she called unsupportive and unproductive disciplinary measures. She also believed that her ability to speak Korean with her parents did not improve her ability to communicate with them about her daily experience:

> I think that pressure from parents could help out, but usually it turns out to be something that motivates the kids to do something worse. A lot of things that Korean parents do to discipline their kids are not working, I guess. I find that what parents do sometimes are not supportive at all—actually opposite—and it makes the kids want to go out and have their fun and forget what their parents are saying. Like, I don't talk to my mom about school or stuff; I usually talk to an older Korean person who could communicate with me. Usually if I need help, I look for an older figure, but not my mother or uncle. Like, even if I could speak fluent Korean, she could never understand the cultural stuff.

Often the cultural gap between second-generation students and their immigrant parents translated into problems on multiple levels for the children, all pointing to a sense of conflict that thrust them into the arms of their friends and other mentors. Hence, the students' peer-network support at school provided not only important schooling information but also equally important emotional support, helping the students to deal with parental conflicts and academic pressures.

BECOMING AMERICAN: CLASS, RACE, AND ETHNICITY

Social constructs such as race and ethnic identity are subject to change, contradiction, and variability within specific contexts. In different social contexts, the Korean American students in this study learned to redefine and reconstruct their racial and ethnic identities as a way to organize their needs, strategies, and interests. Moving away from an essentialist paradigm that positions immigrant experiences as a dichotomy between "original" (nativism) and "American" (assimilation) culture, the Korean American students at MH, with assistance from their peers, learned to negotiate and reconstruct distinct new cultures and subcultures, where their identities were multiple, hybrid, and situational depending on given social and economic contexts (Espiritu, 1994).

The students' comments illustrated the changing and multiple meanings associated with the term *American*. For instance, rather than view themselves as either Korean or American, students often saw themselves as both, where racial identities shifted with changing social context. Mary, a senior at MH, described her experience in this way:

> I was born here, so I am definitely American in some way, but I am, of course, Korean. . . . Even if I am born here, I look definitely Asian or Korean or whatever, and, like, the way my parents live and the way we are, we are not Americanized. . . . If I compare myself to some of my friends, I am more American. They were born there [Korea] and raised there. . . . I would never consider myself just American. Sometimes, if someone teased me or something, I just wanted and would have been happier if I was American, if I looked American. You know how Asians, they look totally different. So I guess if I looked American, no one would tease me and stuff.

However, as evident in Mary's comments, despite the fluidity of identities, as racial minorities, the Korean American students were also subject to racism and categorization imposed on them, operating within a hierarchically racialized system that labeled them as "foreigners" and non-Americans, where Whiteness continues to be the dominant and invisible norm for defining who is "American."

As a way of pointing to their racial minority status, my informants often argued that they did not "look American," nor did they live with "American" parents, who typically represented White middle-class families in the suburbs. Students' experience with racial discrimination and name-calling were often reminders of their racial minority status and lack of control over the production of images about themselves. Some students, when faced with racism, wished that they looked "American" so they did not have to address the accompanying shame and anger.

Not surprisingly, in the magnet high school urban context, where approximately half the student population was Asian American, the students infrequently felt the stigma of being labeled as "Asian." As one student explained, "Now, since I am going to this school, and a lot of people are Asian, I think being Asian is good. I would never want to be like someone else." In fact, my informants said they rarely faced racial discrimination or name-calling within the school—usually, it was on their way home from school (either on the subway or in their neighborhood parks) or when they left their racially diverse urban environment and ventured into the White homogeneity of rural or suburban areas. For instance, Lucy related her experience in a restaurant in an all-White community in Rhode Island. She explained how restaurant personnel refused to serve her and her cousins:

> When I was in Rhode Island, it was all-White community; we never saw Black people or Asian people. We wanted to get food at a restaurant—I think it was me and my cousins—and, like, they wouldn't serve us. They said, "Oh, just hold on a minute." And we waited half an hour. All the people around us were getting food, and when we were leaving, they were calling us chinks and stuff, and kind of saying something like, "Get out of our town," or something. "We don't need your kind," and stuff. I just got so pissed off; we just left. We were waiting, like, 45 minutes, and it's a small restaurant. We were sitting right there, and they wouldn't serve us.

Being seen as a foreigner and non-American, despite having been born and raised in the United States, was a painful and infuriating experience for Lucy:

> My parents are always facing discrimination—like, people say, "This is America, go back to your country," you know, "We don't need you here." I got really pissed off at the restaurant because . . . I really don't think the color of your skin matters, and I hate stereotypes 'cause they don't really have anything to do with the real person. I especially got pissed off when they were saying go back home and stuff. I mean, I was born here. I am a part of America, too.

The students' experiences illustrated how as a racially marginalized group, Asian Americans are often seen as "foreigners" or "immigrants" by outsiders, despite the long history of Asians living in the United States (Chan, 1991; Takaki, 1989). Throughout most of their history in the United States, Asian Americans were consistently denied naturalization and citizenship rights because of racism and fear of economic competition—this despite their having been recruited as a cheap source of labor on an as-needed basis. The way the U.S. mainstream views and treats Asian Americans today finds its roots in this historical exclusion (i.e., denial of citizenship and civil rights). Despite the "open-door" policy of the Immigration Act of 1965, vestiges of this exclusion remain in the form of the historically rooted image of Asian Americans as non-Americans and immigrants (Lowe, 1996).

In addition to feeling excluded, students commented on the tendency of others to stereotype all Asians as "Chinese." This emphasis on Asian homogeneity only exacerbated the students' alienation. Ellen described the frustration that she felt when people automatically assumed she was Chinese:

> I hate it when other people say, "Are you Chinese?" That's the first thing they ask. I hate it because it's racist. It doesn't feel right. They think we all look alike. . . . Nobody would look at me and say I am American, 'cause I just don't look American. A typical American person is Caucasian.

As Ellen's comment illustrates, Asian Americans' ethnicity often becomes racialized, and that racialization serves to marginalize them. The assumption that all Asians fall into one ethnic group reflects what Omi and Winant (1986) called the process of "racial formation," whereby various elements of ethnic identity take on racial meaning and form, while any distinctiveness of specific ethnic identities becomes lost or ignored.

Winnie, a sophomore at MH, described incidents in which strangers asked her "what" she is, as a way of inquiring about her ethnic background. Her comments exemplified the normative paradigm still operating in the United States, in which Whites are spared from being considered a "racial group," while minorities, including Asian Americans, are consistently racialized:

> When I am with my friends at a party or something, and people would come up to me and say, "What are you?" I would be like, I am Korean. And, of course, my friends, who are White—they leave them alone. I feel annoyed 'cause, you know, I think it's really not that important and it's, like, "*What* are you?" is really rude. 'Cause my friends, you know, also have backgrounds, too, you know, not just me. I think you could ask them, too.

Winnie's experience underscored the salience of race and power operating in the United States and how ethnicity for racial minorities takes on a different set of meanings than it does for Whites. For instance, research shows that third- and fourth-generation descendents of White European immigrants operate under "symbolic ethnicity" (Alba, 1990; Gans, 1979; Waters, 1990) and are able to choose their ethnic identities based on subjective attachments to ethnic symbols—a process that is intermittent, voluntary, and noncommittal in character. However, racial minorities do not always have the option of choosing their ethnicity or highlighting particular elements of their ancestry as readily (Espiritu, 1994; Kibria, 2002; Tuan, 1998; Waters, 1990). Far from being "symbolic" or "voluntary" in character, their ethnicity is often imposed on them as a result of systemic racial discrimination and hierarchical power relations.

Interestingly, when I inquired about other racial minorities and their experiences of racial discrimination, my MH informants believed that Blacks and Hispanics faced more egregious stereotyping than Asians, who are often seen as a model minority. Gina explained:

> Yeah, I think, particularly, Blacks and Hispanics. . . . I think they have it more difficult than I do. I mean, there is always a huge stereotype of them, which actually is a lot meaner than stereotypes placed on Korean people . . . that they are not as intelligent and are more violent and that they are not as hardworking. And that Koreans are all perfectionists and smart and they try too hard.

At the same time, some students were careful to point out that as Asian Americans, they often felt invisible—a racial minority absent altogether from racial discourse. In the context of a polarized Black and White racial discourse, some students believed that the United States failed to address various struggles and barriers faced by many Asian Americans. Kyung alluded to media representation as a point of reference:

> Everybody faces discrimination. Asians are total minorities . . . like, if you watch the news, it's either about the Blacks or the Whites, you know. We are sort of outsiders . . . Blacks blame Whites for the bad things that are happening to them. Whites blame the Blacks for their neighborhoods.

As illustrated, the Korean students at MH were keenly aware of racial divisions and how discrimination affected various groups differently. They were also aware of the racial and socioeconomic divide between their neighborhood, punctuated by urban tenement buildings occupied by recent immigrants and racial minorities, and the world of "American" families, marked by suburban houses owned by wealthy Whites beyond the Long Island Expressway:

> When you imagine American, it's like that family with a good-looking father and a good-looking wife and live in a good place. They lead a very good life. Kids are very well off, they get good grades, there is a baby. There is a guy, a girl, and a baby. They live in Long Island or somewhere with their white picket fence. They really lead a good life . . . the White people . . . the White family.

These divides cast a long shadow over the students' lives, blunting even their hard-earned success to some degree. Many of the students I interviewed believed that even with economic and social support from their parents and ethnic communities, and the prospect of good careers and long-term economic success born of investment in education, they would never be considered

"American" by the larger society because of their racial minority status. Suh Na explained:

> My parents want me to have a better life than they have now, 'cause they work really hard to earn money, and they want me to have a better and easier life where I could take days off during holidays and weekends, and work less and earn more money. I help them out on Saturdays, and it's hard work, and I feel it every time I work. So I think, I should have a better life. . . . But I think that even if you are Americanized, your appearance tells you that you are Asian, Korean, and Chinese, or whatever, so I don't think you will ever get over that wall.

EDUCATION AS A RACIAL STRATEGY

As illustrated, the Korean American students at MH were painfully aware of how their racial minority status might be used to marginalize them as foreigners or non-American, despite their having been born and raised in the United States. However, embedded in strong social support at home, communities, and school, the Korean students had learned to use education as a means to, in part, withstand the stigma accompanying their racial minority status. Underlying this process was a firm belief that to compensate for their racial minority status, they had to work even harder and excel in school. In other words, for the Korean American students at MH, education represented what Kibria (2002) referred to as a "racial strategy." She argued, "Their parents suggested that academic achievement was a way of overcoming the racial exclusion and barriers in the United States, of 'making it' in spite of them" (p. 54). According to most of the Korean American students at MH, their parents emphasized the importance of using education to compensate for racial barriers facing Asian Americans in the United States. Yun Shin, a junior at MH, repeated her mother's advice:

> My mom would want me to be Americanized and get education, since there is so much racism against Asians and stuff, but she wants me to keep my Korean culture. Being American never entered my mind. It's not that I don't want to be, but it's just that I've never been accepted as one, never been considered one, so I never thought of myself as one. Because I am always surrounded by Asians, being American never entered my mind. You know, if I say, "I am American," they would say, "No, you are not. You are Asian."

By placing Asian American students' educational aspirations in the context of historical exclusion, Hirschman and Wong (1986), Mark and Chih

(1982), and Sue and Okazaki (1990) have explained that exigencies of discrimination in noneducational settings has led Asian Americans to view education as a functional means of social and economic mobility. Similarly, Suzuki (1980) has argued that because Asian Americans have been historically excluded from the mainstream labor market and forced into self-employment, first-generation parents have emphasized using education to achieve career opportunities in mainstream economy.

Moreover, many of the students explained how their parents warned them of racial discrimination and made them aware of their racial minority status. According to the students, their parents reiterated the significance of learning skills necessary to achieve in school while maintaining strong ethnic ties. As Kim commented:

> My parents think that it's, like, going to be a White-populated society, so, like, they keep telling me to try my best and stuff, and just be aware that they are there and you are going to face some discrimination. Not try to fit into their society, but know about your surrounding and stuff.

The students' responses echo findings from earlier studies that have shown how children of immigrants, particularly those residing in poor, isolated neighborhoods, need close ties to their immigrant parents' ethnic enclaves and communities to withstand class and racial inequality (Caplan, Choy, & Whitmore, 1991; Gibson, 1988; Portes & Rumbaut, 1996; Zhou & Bankston, 1996, 1998). Gibson (1988) described this as a strategy of accommodation or selective assimilation—a process whereby the children in the Punjabi community learned skills necessary to be competitive in American society but resisted assimilating with the lower-SES White community in which they resided. Additional studies on Southeast Asian refugee students also indicate that their academic success was primarily attributable to their close ties to their first-generation parental ethnic networks and their ability to resist downward assimilation into their surrounding poor, minority communities (Caplan et al., 1991; Zhou & Bankston, 1996, 1998).

The capacity to resist the alienating effects of class and racial discrimination depends on the embeddedness in family and community networks of support (Gottlieb, 1991). Raising minority and immigrant children involves strategies by which families and community members struggle to equip and strengthen their children so they can negotiate conflicting relations and worlds—and acquire a measure of resilience in the process (Boykin, 1986; Boykin & Toms, 1985; Neisser, 1986; Phelan et al., 1993). In order to believe in and use education as an effective means of social mobility, minority children need to learn to cross borders, overcome barriers, and resist the effects of exclusionary forces. The Korean students at MH certainly illustrated the importance of developing resilience through ties with protective social networks within their home and community and at school.

To summarize, students negotiated their racial and ethnic identities according to the social and economic context. At the same time, racial minority students saw their racial identities ascribed to them in the form of exclusionary stereotypes and false constructs of homogeneity. Protected with strong social capital at home, communities, and school, however, the MH students learned to use education as a racial strategy. That is, they firmly upheld the belief that as racial minorities, they would have to work even harder in school to obtain the economic parity with White Americans. As illustrated, the Korean American students typically associated being "American" with Whiteness; however, their comments also illustrate the changing and complex meaning associated with being "American." For the Korean American students at MH, the belief that education would pave the way for obtaining the *economic status* of middle-class Americans was strong; however, they nevertheless were keenly aware that despite their middle-class economic status, they might not necessarily be accepted *racially* as Americans. This predicament highlights the multiple and situational meanings associated with being American, the salience of race, and the integral and complex relationship between race and class in the United States.

CHAPTER 5

Korean American High School Dropouts: Overcoming Institutional Barriers

> I learned nothing. Nothing! Do you know how loud those kids are? I can't even listen to anyone. Teachers, they don't teach you, like nothing. Usually if teachers teach you, students make a lot of noise, a lot of noise; they will throw garbage and everything . . . Teachers can't teach properly, and I can't hear anything because kids talk a lot in class . . . teachers don't have any control.
>
> —John, age 18

POOR, ISOLATED URBAN HIGH SCHOOLS: LIMITED SCHOOLING AND GUIDANCE SUPPORT

While Korean American students at MH were embedded in supportive networks at home, in their communities, and at school composed of individuals who provided institutional support regarding schooling, the Korean American high school dropouts navigated through schooling alone, isolated and disconnected from institutional agents who could provide important schooling support. In contrast to the Korean American students at MH, who attended an academic school populated mostly by middle-class White and Asian students, the dropouts attended low-performing public high schools with academic standing below the city average, faced with limited resources, and populated mostly by low-income Black, Hispanic, and Asian students. Consequently, the dropouts faced myriad institutional obstacles to building relationships with key gatekeepers and accumulating social capital toward achieving in school.

Poor communities are at a disadvantage in gaining access to and building social capital. The more affluent communities not only have greater financial and human capital resources, but they also have access to funded public institutions, like schools, that reproduce, if not advance, their economic position. On the other hand, the residents of poor communities may have strong networks within their neighborhoods, but those neighbors are not able to provide them with connections and references to high-paying jobs. Moreover, their public institutions, such as schools, are poorly funded and isolated. With these limited resources, they are more likely to focus on overcoming institutional obstacles rather than advancing economic and political opportunities (Saegert et al., 2001).

Throughout the interviews, my informants spoke of attending high schools offering ineffective learning environments and few opportunities for constructing relationships with teachers and counselors who could help students with schooling. The Korean American high school dropouts explained repeatedly that even when they tried to learn in school, classes were often too loud and disorganized for any meaningful learning to take place. Robert, 17 at the time of this study and born in the United States, confided that because the school environment was not conducive to learning, leaving school would be a better use of his time and energy:

> I would go to the classes, but then my patience would run thin, and I would just get tired. Or I would go to class, but the kids are so rowdy that I can't learn, and the teacher won't teach. If I don't learn anything, there is no point of me being there. And I eventually just left. 'Cause if I came to school, I wanted to do something, not just sit there.

As earlier studies have shown, dropping out of school is but the final stage in a cumulative process of school disengagement, where students' educational engagement is associated with the extrinsic rewards of schoolwork as well as the intrinsic rewards associated with the curriculum and educational activities. Students' school membership is also associated with their commitment to and trust in the institution, belief in the legitimacy of schooling, and social ties to other students, teachers, and counselors who can guide them through schooling (Natriello et al., 1990; Newmann, Wehlage, & Lamborn, 1992; Rumberger & Larson, 1998, Wehlage & Rutter, 1986).

Given the limited structural resources available in these poorly funded and overcrowded urban schools, teachers and counselors also face tremendous obstacles in being able to provide schooling support for their students. The students I interviewed felt firsthand the effects of these structural problems in the educational system. In such school environments, students consistently mentioned the lack of academic rigor and limited academic and social support from teachers and counselors. Jung Suh, 18 at the time of the study and born in the United States, described his experience at a school characterized by low expectations and mutual disrespect between teachers and students:

> The thing about New York school, as to why I lost the passion to learn, or whatever, is because first of all, I don't like the teachers, how they treat you . . . I mean, a good teacher can make a bad subject worthwhile. And I came here, and it's not like that. They all think you are ignorant, and they talk to you like you are ignorant, and honestly, it just pisses me off. I didn't want to stay there, and personally, I don't like being looked down upon and seen as if I am stupid. And that's very offensive to me, so I just left. And it's not just seeing it happen to me, I don't like it seeing it happen to others, too.

Although most of the Korean American dropouts spoke of schooling experiences marked by uncaring relationships with teachers and counselors, some spoke of adults at the school, including teachers, counselors, and even security guards, who were in their corner urging them to stop cutting classes and associating with friends at school who "bring people down." Emily, who was 19 years old and born in the United States, recalled her experience:

> Yeah, they [teachers and counselors] liked me and my dad, and they tried to help me and my dad to see that staying in school would be better for me. Like, setting up schedule to help me; and if I left school, they would call my dad 'cause they didn't want him to be worried. My friends would cut, but then when I tried to cut, the guards would stop me and say, "Go to class. Why are you doing this? Why are you trying to ruin your life? You would be disappointing your dad. I wouldn't say this to everyone, but you should be around much better people. These people bring themselves down, so they will bring other people down." So, people cared about me and wanted me to do well.

Despite the existence of these caring adults in her school, Emily navigated through schooling alone, failed to seek their help or guidance, and eventually stopped coming to school. Her experience illustrated that even though low-income minority students may be embedded in networks of families, peers, and school agents who care about them, they often fail to seek help from others and are, to the contrary, likely to navigate through schooling alone with little support (Stanton-Salazar, 2001). Those students who are alienated from schools, in particular, face fear, anger, distrust, and loss of confidence in the support process and, therefore, are less likely to seek help from teachers and counselors (Phelan et al., 1993). Poor, minority students face numerous institutional obstacles that prevent them from the constructing kinds of relationships and social networks that provide access to important forms of institutional support.

INSTITUTIONAL BARRIERS TO ACCESSING SCHOOLING AND INSTITUTIONAL RESOURCES

Obstacles to Building Relationships with Teachers and Counselors

The overall poor relationships with teachers and counselors reiterated by my informants, however, cannot be understood adequately without examining the larger social forces that schools are subjected to. Schools are increasingly facing pressure from federal and state agencies to improve their performance, and assessment is based largely on standardized exams and graduation rates. When such mandates are handed down without providing adequate structural resources to meet these standards, there is less incentive to help the most needy students in the school system. Studies have shown that in the face of such testing and assessment policies, schools have resorted to "pushing out" students who are "at risk" in order to improve school performance. That is, the panopoly of high-stakes testing could result in adverse outcomes, such as increase in rates of high school dropouts and "push-outs" (Orfield, Losen, Wald, & Swanson, 2004).

In line with this, numerous Korean American high school dropouts interviewed spoke of their receiving inadequate counseling, and some confided that they were advised to leave school and encouraged to take the GED exam instead. According to some of the students, counselors advised that they had a better chance of getting a high school diploma if they left school, given the students' lack of interest, excessive absences, low academic achievement, and likelihood of not graduating on time (see also Fine, 1991). What is notable, and unfortunate, in these cases is that students were neither adequately informed about the range of choices afforded them nor fully cognizant of how a GED might be different from a high school diploma. When I interviewed Hee Kyung, he was 18 years old and had dropped out of high school more than a year before. He explained:

> When I met my counselor, she said I should take the GED and not go back to school. I thought the GED and high school diploma were the same. I wanted to leave the school, and when I left, I felt better.

Like Hee Kyung, other Korean high school dropouts said they were encouraged to drop out of high school and/or take the GED, instead of receiving accurate information and the necessary resources to graduate from high school (Bowdith, 1993; Fine, 1991; Rumberger & Larson, 1998). Unfortunately, these systemic institutional problems caused many of the Korean American dropouts to see their counselors as authority figures who ultimately did not care about their welfare. These hostilities and disincentives to graduate—partly as the result of misinformation—left students feeling bereft of advisers who could guide them through a difficult process. Consequently, the students exhibited anger, frustration, and mistrust toward their teachers and counselors. As Sam explained:

> The counselor was the one who kicked me out. First of all, I am not supposed to get kicked out . . . a couple of my friends got her for counseling, and she was really mean. All of them got kicked out. She will give me attitude. She'll say, "Oh, you again? Just leave the school." Just like that. That's why I decided to leave. I don't care.

Theresa, one of the program administrators of the GED program at YCC, confirmed this trend, for the organization had witnessed it throughout the New York City public schools. She explained that because the schools were crowded and under pressure to increase graduation rates and test scores, many teachers and counselers resorted to "pushing out" students who might need their support the most:

> It's easier for the school system to say to these kids, "Leave the school system, you'll be better off." Even though they are legally allowed to stay in school till they are 21, no one ever wants to stay in school till they are 21, and the schools don't encourage it because they are overcrowded, and the fewer students, the better for them. They want to keep that graduation rate high. It affects the test scores. It affects the way the school looks if they have students who are over the age of 18.

According to Mike, the program director of the GED program at YCC, these problems had become even more acute since the New York City schools implemented a requirement that all students take and pass Regents Exams in order to graduate. This standard has in some cases encouraged recent immigrant students with language barriers to drop out of high school and take the GED, all the while believing that this alternate route would be quicker and easier than enduring 4 years of high school. Implementation of these higher standards without adequate language assistance for recent immigrant children is one of the biggest challenges faced by some schools. Mike continued:

> You do have the more recent immigrants that do have serious language problems, and that's a big reason they drop out. And the Regents is a very, very big reason—an obstacle that most of them can't overcome. I don't know when, but year by year they added a new section and new test as requirements. You need to pass it. Now it's almost all subjects. So for a recent immigrant who came let's say

> 2, 3 years ago that tried to pass a very difficult English test, they would realize that no matter how much I study, I am just not going to be able to pass this test. So they go, "Oh, I heard GED is easier, so I'll take it that way."

These comments from the Korean American high school dropouts have important implications for the rise in the number of students taking the GED in recent years. According to a recent report by the Urban Institute on the GED (Chaplin, 1999), there has been a steady increase of students opting to take the GED rather than graduate with a high school diploma. It is estimated that in 1967, approximately 150,000 people received a GED in the United States, but by 1998 this number had increased to almost 500,000, with about 200,000 of these recipients under the age of 20. The percent of GED recipients steadily rose from 2% in 1954 to over 14% by 1987 (Cameron & Heckman, as cited in Chaplin, 1999). Moreover, an increasing number of GED recipients are as young as 16, further diverting teenagers away from obtaining a traditional high school diploma. However, as Chaplin (1999) illustrated, there is ample evidence showing the labor-market costs of obtaining a GED instead of a high school diploma. That is, dropping out of high school to get a GED results in substantially lower income and earning later in life. Teenagers who are opting to take a GED instead of graduating from high school—as well as their parents—should be well informed of these findings *before* making the decision to drop out of high schools.

Transferring from One Ineffective School to Another

Because their schools failed to adequately serve the most needy Korean American high school dropouts, and in some cases encouraged them to leave, many dropouts corroborated their working-class parents' strategy by transferring to different schools, often as a way of resisting difficult conditions but also as a way of running from their own problems. In many cases, this strategy was as self-defeating as it was self-fulfilling. Not only did the high mobility rate create more problems than it solved, but some Korean American dropouts transferred so frequently that they struggled to remember the long list of public schools they had attended. For instance, Rob attended a different high school almost every semester for a span of 3½ years before finally dropping out:

> I dropped out of OH. I was a student there for half a year, or one term. Before then, I was at FS for another half a year. And before I got to FS, I was at NH for a little over half a year. Before that, I started out at BS, where I was at the longest . . . 2½ years.

Hoping ultimately to graduate, Rob nevertheless struggled with numerous challenges at each high school. His long journey toward earning a diploma, which never happened, illustrates how difficult it was for him to adjust to and build relationships at each school. The process left him further isolated and alienated from the schooling process:

> After I got to NH, I was doing fine, and if I would have stayed there, I would have graduated on time. But after being exposed to so many people around you, after I got to NH, I was really isolated from the group. It was hard to fit in as a new person. So I decided to take my senior year to come back. You know, to study here. That was probably like the worst thing I ever did. After I got back to FS, I messed up extremely bad.

With his haphazard school record and short a few credits to graduate, he transferred yet again so that he could "get it over with" as quickly as possible and earn his diploma. But faced with escalating family problems and alienated from the schooling process, he dropped out shortly thereafter:

> So then, like, I transferred to OH because OH is supposed to be like a Mickey Mouse course; get you credits and graduate. So I went to OH, and it was so easy that I just wasn't interested. So then I didn't go to OH. And then, like, I needed around seven, five credits after NH, and when I got to FS I got one credit, and then I got two credits from OH, so I needed two more credits to graduate. It was basically, like, I just want to get it over with. I was dealing a lot of stuff from home also. I didn't want to really deal with it. So I just, like, tried to get the easy way out of getting my credits.

As Rob's experience illustrates, because of shifting environments, standards, and expectations, children who frequently transfer schools face a number of challenges in adjusting both socially and academically (Holland, Kaplan, & Davis, 1974; Lee & Burkham, 1992). Students are less likely to put down roots in their schools or communities and build the trusting relationships with teachers and friends that are crucial for accumulating and building social capital. Additionally, measures of students' social and academic disengagement, such as low grades, misbehavior, high absenteeism, and dropout rates, have all been associated with student mobility—the frequency with which students changed schools. And school and residential mobility were significantly higher among students of lower socioeconomic status than among students of higher socioeconomic status (Rumberger & Larson, 1998).

As mentioned, the high transfer rate among many Korean American dropouts I interviewed was often self-defeating, creating more problems than it solved by ensnaring the students in a downward spiral, until transferring schools gave way to dropping out as the strategy of choice to deal with poor academic records fraught with a high rate of suspension, failing grades, absences, and class cutting (Natriello, 1986; Natriello et al., 1990). Students explained that once they began cutting classes, they couldn't quite make up for their failing grades, which in turn discouraged them from attending classes. When they tried going back to school, they were so far behind that they couldn't catch up with schoolwork. This further increased the likelihood of their disengagement with school.

John dropped out of high school after having been in numerous schools for 3 years. He explained that, although he aspired to do well in school, after repeatedly cutting classes with his friends, he found it more difficult to go back to school:

> In the beginning, I enjoyed going to school. I am going to do well, this and that. But after a while, I cut a few days and then I wouldn't want to go back to school, and I would cut even more. And then when I go back, the teachers will be there, grill me this and that, or whatever. But then after that, I will keep going and then, I will lose the feel to go to school and don't want to go anymore. You know, nothing was really holding me in school, and I lost the will to stay.

Students admitted that after missing so many days of school, it became difficult to go back to school and "catch up," which made it increasingly easier to drop out. As John explained, cutting classes gave him a chance to avoid some of the problems he was facing in school:

> You know, it's the simplest way to get a little bit. You cut school, and then you don't have to think about it. The school really doesn't care whether you go or not. I didn't care either. I thought, if I go to school, I will get into fights or made fun of, or didn't understand what they were doing, so why bother going to school? That's what I thought. And after you cut 1 month, you can't go back to school. You don't understand what they are talking about. If you want to catch up, you have to work really hard.

When I asked John if he had reached out to teachers or counselors at school for guidance, he reiterated the lack of caring relationships, mistrust, and overall isolation in navigating through the schooling system:

> I didn't have a relationship with teachers. I didn't really want their help and wanted to do it on my own. Guidance counselors tried to help, but I didn't like the way they did it. Like, once I didn't go to

> school for 2 months, and then I decided to go back to school. The guidance counselor called, and she kind of put me down and didn't encourage me. Like, she would say, if I kept this up I would get kicked out of school and not get a high school diploma. I don't really show them my feelings. I said, "OK."

The lack of caring relationships between counselors and students is clearly illustrated in the Korean students' schooling experiences. Researchers have shown the significance of caring teachers, counselors, and peers in schools, and how such relationships can initiate and build relationships that convey acceptance and confirmation of the students' investment in and contribution to the school community (Noddings, 1992; Stanton-Salazar, 2001; Valenzuela 1999). For instance, Valenzuela (1999) argued that the existence of caring teachers in the school community played an important role in Mexican American students' ability to build social capital in schools.

Students' comments also show that in the context of such limited resources at home and in schools, the students find it difficult to connect their academic aspirations and achievement. Providing students with institutional and social support, such as access to caring teachers and counselors, is pivotal for bridging this gap and achieving academic success (Croninger & Lee, 2001; Stanton-Salazar, 2001; Valenzuela, 1999). However, according to Korean dropouts in the study, they were not privy to such relationships. Given their school contexts, the Korean high school dropouts did not have access to important and caring relationships with teachers or counselors who might have been able to help them complete and excel in high school.

The dropouts' testimony also reveals, among other things, that school violence and racial harassment contribute to school disengagement and, ultimately, to dropping out. In fact, racial harassment and school fights occurred daily, and for the Korean American dropouts, the violence during or after school only increased their likelihood of getting suspended and dropping out. In the case of Jung Suh, fighting in and outside of school was a typical affair throughout his junior high and high school years. When I asked him whether he got into fights in school, he replied:

> Nothing that I couldn't take care of. I don't know, usually stupid kids, who try to act tough. They will be grillin' [*sic*] me and when I grill back, they say what are you staring at? So if they want to fight, I fight. It's not like I am looking for trouble, it's like if they come to me and like they are going to be retarded. If anything, I don't like to fight.

Even though Jung Suh would have preferred not to fight, he further explained how important it was to stand up for himself in these situations because he refused to be disrespected. These incidences, however, were not limited to his peers but extended to his teachers:

> People who think they are big shit, I am sorry but I can't handle that. I was suspended in junior high school for fighting with the teachers . . . This one teacher, who wasn't even my teacher, came into the room and like one day, I didn't have my binder, just my loose leaf, and he was talking about kids who don't bring binders and don't even come to school prepared, they are not going to make it in life. And I am the only one who had that, and I know he was talking to me. So, I just started cursin' [*sic*] at him . . . I was just like, who is he to tell me whether I am going to make it in life or not? And he don't even know me. It's a total disrespect when he don't even know me. My guidance counselors, they didn't care. They would just send me out.

While many students, mostly my male informants, reiterated their experiences of school violence related to racism, disrespect, and peer pressure, other students, mostly my female informants, avoided school altogether for fear of being subject to harassment. For instance, Tina was in tenth grade when she dropped out of high school. She spoke of being in constant fear of verbal and sometimes physical abuse, which a group of girls in her class perpetrated. As the racial slurs and taunting escalated, Tina was left alone to defend herself, without the aid of teachers or other students. She recalled the day a group of girls in the class threw gum at her hair, stole her wallet from her school bag, and followed her home after school. After this incident, she began cutting school until she stopped going to school altogether. Instead of confiding in her parents or seeking help from school personnel, she pretended to go to school for nearly 3 months, ducking into a public library by herself and waiting out the schoolday until 3:00 P.M., when she headed home. She explained the sense of helplessness she experienced, alone and isolated, without support from friends or adults:

> I hated school because all the kids used to tease me. It was better in junior high school, where I had some friends. My first year at high school was fine, but the next year was the worst year. A group of girls in my class who hated me threw gum at my hair and stole my wallet. When I told them to stop, they laughed and kept on calling me names. I dreaded coming to school. Little by little, I stopped coming, and the following year, I dropped out.

Although Tina did not reach out to teachers and counselors for help, the school also failed to intervene against such racial harassment. Tina rarely received help from teachers or counselors when she was faced with such verbal and physical harassment. Her experience serves as a reminder that, like other racial minorities, Asian Americans face racism and discrimination at school and in the workplace. Particularly in schools, teachers and administrators should set zero-tolerance policies for any form of discrimination, whether based on race, gender, disability, or sexual orientation. Moreover, teachers and counselors must actively intervene when witnessing such acts of discrimination and harassment.

SECOND-GENERATION PEER NETWORKS: RESISTING FAILING SCHOOLS THROUGH AN ALTERNATE ROUTE

With limited access to institutional agents and social capital at home or in school, the Korean American high school dropouts were often left alone to defend themselves or to make crucial decisions. This is in contrast to the MH students, who were embedded in networks providing strong social capital at home, in their communities, and in school. In such a social context, the MH students' network revolved around obtaining information and learning skills specifically related to achieving in school and *advancing* their economic status—a strategy that used education as a long-term investment for obtaining social mobility. However, as we have seen, the low-income Korean American high school dropouts' network revolved around a strategy of "getting by" and *overcoming* institutional barriers—gaining short-term jobs, joining the military, and learning about GED programs as a way to address their low socioeconomic status and limited opportunity structure.

Similar to the Korean American students at MH, the Korean American high school dropouts also spoke of associating with Korean peers in school, co-ethnic churches, and neighborhoods. However, unlike the MH students, many of the high school dropouts had Korean friends who also came from low-income families, were high school dropouts, or were in the military. For instance, John dropped out of high school on the advice of an older Korean friend whom he calls *hyung*, or "older brother." He then followed in his Korean friend's footsteps and decided to join the marines:

> A lot of *hyungs*, the older guys, told us about the marines. They are like older brothers. All my friends from high school, we used to go to same church, and then from there, we would meet friends and other friends there. They went to the marines.

Similarly, Sam also learned about joining the army through his *hyung*. He dropped out of high school during his senior year and hoped to join the army shortly thereafter. Since he had no contact with his mother and his father had passed away a few years earlier, he was living with his uncle and aunt when I met him. His government assistance stopped when he turned 18 and he felt the pressure to be financially independent. He was aware that living with his relatives, who were also supporting their own children, might not be an option in the near future. For him, the army provided the hope of getting a free education:

> So, I have this pressure, but it wouldn't have been as great if I still got money from the government. I used to get money from my aunt and uncle to support me, but that doesn't come anymore since I am 18 now, and so there is even more pressure put on me. It's not just me. There are my cousins, and there are six people in the house; so right now, I am gonna have to start working soon. I am planning to go to the marines this summer and then go to college after that. You know, any military in the U.S., you get free education

The choice to drop out of high school and join the military to earn a college degree was not an easy decision for the Korean high school dropouts. Sam confessed that his decision to drop out of high school in his senior year and enter the army was one of the toughest choices that he had had to make. When I asked him if he had talked to adults other than his Korean "brothers" about his decision, he explained that his "brothers" understood him and knew what was best for him. His aunt and uncle did not initially agree with his decision to leave high school, but when Sam explained that he would go on to college after his service in the army, they agreed. Since his aunt and uncle, with their low socioeconomic status as well as limited English-language skills and knowledge of the U.S. education system, could not be of much help, Sam rarely approached them for guidance on schooling or career opportunities. Sam's experience, similar to that of many of the dropouts in this study, pointed to the consistent theme of students having to navigate through the education system primarily on their own, without much adult presence or guidance (Lew, 2004, in press).

In addition to the military option, many Korean American high school dropouts learned about the GED program at YCC through fellow Korean friends. For instance, Dave was 17 years old, had dropped out of high school the year before I met him, and was enrolled in the GED program at YCC. He explained that he had five close Korean friends but that none of them had graduated from high school. He continued: "Because we always hung out and didn't go to school. If you don't go to school once or twice, then it gets harder. You don't have much fun at school, grades are low, so you hang out together. After lunch, we would just cut out and leave school." When I asked Dave whether his friends were also in the GED program, he explained that two of them were, but the others were either working full time or were in the military:

> My closest friends are from the Korean church I go to. I brought them here to the GED program since they dropped out. One girl I know, who is my best friend's girlfriend, is out of school. So I told her about this program and told her to come by. But it's hard because she works full time at a restaurant. Right now, because the owner opened another store at New Jersey, she is running the store there, so she has very little time for school.

Those who were enrolled in the GED program at YCC clearly saw this as an alternate route to college and a chance to start over. Mark repeated a pivotal conversation he had had with his Korean and Chinese friends who had dropped out of high school years earlier. They carefully advised him to take the GED and go on to college:

> I learned about this GED program through my friends, who also dropped out before me. A lot of older brothers, you know, both Korean and Chinese. They were, like, "You dropped out, but do well in GED." They would tell me, like, "You can't go back and change the time or anything, life goes on, so do well in GED and continue to go to college." So, I am trying to start fresh, you know.

The Korean American dropouts who could take the GED route consistently mentioned their belief that this exam was a cure-all—a silver bullet that would erase their delinquent school records and give them a "second chance." Many students believed that the GED would be a quicker and easier process than enduring the weight of academic failure, humiliation, and the disrespect of teachers, counselors, and peers. Although my informants believed that they would need a college education to gain economic opportunities, they were not convinced that 4 years of high school would necessarily be the best means of getting there. In effect, the Korean American dropouts also used the GED as a form of adaptation and resistance to the poor-quality schools and limited economic opportunities they faced.

BECOMING THE "OTHER" KOREAN: CLASS, RACE, AND ETHNICITY

When noting reasons for academic achievement among Korean American students, it is also important to account for their level of trust and faith in mainstream institutions, such as schools, as well as their expectations for social mobility. Students are likely to be involved in the process of self-elimination if there is a lack of access to institutional agents, combined with a perception of discrimination and other societal barriers toward social mobility (Fine, 1991; Fordham & Ogbu, 1986; Gibson & Ogbu, 1991; Ogbu, 1987; Stanton-Salazar, 1997, 2001). Ogbu's research on race and school achievement illustrated how students' cultural frame of reference and their interpretation of economic, social, and political barriers influences their inclination to use education as a means for social mobility. For poor, minority students isolated in urban areas, poor school performance is also a form of adaptation to their limited social and economic opportunity in adult life. Students' social consciousness is built on beliefs shared with significant others and community members. The degree to which one is academically successful depends on one's network as well as one's experience within the socioeconomic opportunity structure in school and society at large (Bourdieu & Passeron, 1977; Ogbu, 1987; Stanton-Salazar, 1997, 2001).

Expanding on Ogbu's (1987) theory of an oppositional cultural frame of reference and "acting White," an increasing number of studies have complicated the dichotomy of voluntary and involuntary groups' experiences by illustrating how members of both groups learn to adopt oppositional cultural frames of reference (Portes & Rumbaut, 1996, 2001; Waters, 1994, 1999). These studies show that children of immigrants who live in poor, isolated neighborhoods without the protection of strong familial networks and social capital are likely to assimilate the cultures and norms of their poor, minority peers and adopt an oppositional cultural frame of reference that may not be conducive to schooling success.

Absent from this scholarly discussion, however, is how low-income and low-achieving children of Asian immigrants, without the protection of strong social networks, may be negotiating their racial and ethnic identities, and how this process may be similar to and different from that of other racial groups. The following section will begin to examine some of these questions.

As illustrated, in addition to having limited access to social and economic support from their immigrant parents and co-ethnic communities, the Korean American dropouts received limited support in school—urban schools mostly populated by poor minorities and recent immigrants and plagued by violence and high dropout rates. In this school context, the low-income Korean American dropouts rarely came into contact with wealthy Whites; instead, most of their peers were Asians, Blacks, and Hispanics of low socioeconomic status. The racial and economic isolation of these youngsters, therefore, perpetuated their distrust of and alienation from wealthy Whites. Henry, age 19 at the time of the study and born in Korea, explained that he and his friends had very little contact with wealthy Whites, either in school or in their neighborhoods, and that they saw Whites largely through an oppositional lens:

> I feel closer to Blacks and Hispanics than Whites. I think most Koreans are closer to Black culture. It's not like I hate Whites, but I don't like them either. When I see a White person, I don't see them as just a person. I see them as a White person. When I see them, I think, "I don't know you, I don't know what you do, and I don't want to get to know you." My friends don't like Whites either, 'cause we sometimes get into fights with Whites and the way they talk about White people. When I see a White person, the first thing I think about is that they are rich and educated, and most of Koreans like me are not educated and rich. So when I see them, I think they are from another planet.

Other Korean American high school dropouts in this study also were keenly aware of the stark difference between them and wealthier Whites and, by extension, their own racial minority and low socioeconomic status. Their daily experience was restricted to a particular community and neighborhood that taught them many "facts of life": that their family and friends, mostly racial minorities of low-income backgrounds, lived in poor housing projects; that adults worked in menial jobs or were unemployed; and that their friends did not achieve in school.

In addition to distinguishing themselves from Whiteness, my informants also distinguished themselves from the "wealthy" Korean and other Asian Americans who grew up in middle-class homes and privileged neighborhoods. Emily, 19 and born in the United States, explained how such "wealthy" Korean Americans from better neighborhoods would not understand her experience and struggles of growing up in housing projects populated largely by poor Blacks and Hispanics:

> This Korean girl I know at church was brought up in Bayside, which is mostly White and Asian. If she was brought up in Philadelphia, it would be different. For me, where I lived, majority of the people were Hispanics and Blacks. She doesn't know the environment I grew up in. I know their culture and the way they work. She only knows what she knows. It's mixed, but they are wealthier, and they live in houses. We struggled, and she grew up more comfortable. You know, where I grew up, everybody worked to make a living, the houses were dirty, lived in one bedroom with four people in it. You know, that's how I lived. One bedroom with my mother, father, brother, and me.

Emily continued to explain that her low social and economic status represented a kind of collective "minority" experience that distinguished her from the wealthier and privileged Whites and Asians:

> We went through a lot living in that environment. She [wealthy Korean American friend] doesn't know a lot about that. She is more to the Whites and Asians, and I am more to the Blacks and Hispanics, more toward the minority.

Similarly, in her study of second-generation Korean American adults in New York City, Lee (2004) has shown that while middle-class Koreans touted their ethnicity and model minority status as reasons for their achievement, working-class Koreans interpreted their experiences as shaped largely by their class position. In the context of an ethnic community that is predominantly middle class and socially mobile, the working-class Korean Americans, in order to "save face" from being "looked down" upon, tend to distance themselves somewhat from Korean communities at large and downplay their ethnicity (Lee, 2004).

This study further shows, however, that as the Korean American high school dropouts distinguished themselves from their co-ethnic peers along class lines, they also distinguished themselves from more educated or "studious" Koreans. Ken, 18 and born in the United States, explained that he had many Korean American friends whom he had met in Korean churches, clubs, or schools. But he carefully distinguished himself from the "studious" Koreans and explained that while his Korean American friends "hang out" after church, the "studious" Koreans go home after school with their family:

> I don't hang out with anyone else but Koreans. I used to hang out at the Elmhurst Park a lot. I used to play basketball there, and when you play sports there you meet people, and then you meet their friends. The basketball thing was always after the [church] service. Those kinds of people, you know, the studious people who don't go out much, would leave right after the service. So, you know who they are.

Moreover, Ken aligned "studious" and "wealthy" Koreans with Whiteness because of the way they spoke, dressed, and succeeded in school:

> They [studious Koreans] live a different world. Totally different. When I look at them, I never had a friend like them, so I don't know. When I see them, it's like I am seeing a White person. They never cut school, they use a different language, they use proper language, and I use slangs. They dress more simple; some try to show off, but they don't care what other people think. Their hairstyles are different. Most of them are like Whites because they don't know this kind of life, and they hang out with Whites, and most of the time they don't hang out anyway.

In effect, the findings here show that working-class Korean American high school dropouts define the dominant society more broadly. In addition to distinguishing themselves from wealthy Whites, the dropouts also distinguished themselves from socially mobile Koreans and other Asians whom they deemed "wealthy and studious"—attributes of "success" they associated with Whiteness. In the process, most of the dropouts aligned their shared experiences of racism and low socioeconomic status with those of their low-income minority peers—Blacks, Hispanics, and Asians.

In this respect, the dropouts' experiences illustrate how they both internalized and resisted the dominant ideology that attributes "success" to Whites and Asians but "failure" to Blacks and Hispanics: While they de-racialized "successful" and "wealthy" Koreans and Asians by associating them with Whiteness, they also resisted Whiteness themselves by aligning their own racial and economic status with other "minorities" of color. That is, while they bought into the model minority stereotype by associating upwardly mobile Koreans with Whiteness, they also resisted the dominant ideology by disassociating themselves from these same upwardly mobile Koreans and aligning with Blacks and Hispanics, whom they saw as monolithically poor and disenfranchised.

In a society based on a polarized discourse of success and failure, rich and poor, and Black and White, students struggled to make sense of their distinctive experience, one marked by racial minority and low socioeconomic status. Their comments also claimed a space within a polarized racial discourse that tolerates Asians as either "near-Whites" or invisible minorities whose experiences are often de-racialized and de-contextualized. Okihiro (1994), for instance, explained that within the Black-and-White racial paradigm, Asians, American Indians, and Latinos are defined in relation to acting either White or Black. The racial paradigm of being "near-Whites" or "just like Blacks" is historically and socially constructed. Okihiro (1994) stated, "The construct is historicized, within the progressive tradition of American history, to show the evolution of Asians from minority to majority status, or 'from hardship and discrimination to become a model of self-respect and achievement in today's America' " (p. 33). Yet Okihiro (1994) argued that Asian Americans have been marginalized throughout U.S. history, as the labels of "near-Blacks" in the past or "near-Whites" in the present demonstrate.

Meanwhile, embedded in students' comments is also the implicit marginalization they experience *within* the Korean community. To be poor and uneducated within a community that is predominantly middle class, college educated, and upwardly mobile also means being looked down on and being excluded. As a means of developing survival strategies to endure and resist such marginalization within their own co-ethnic communities, as well as of withstanding institutional barriers such as inferior schooling, economic limitation, and racial discrimination within the larger society, the working-class Korean American high school dropouts formed cultural frames of reference and social identities in opposition to the dominant society (Gibson & Ogbu, 1991; Matute-Bianchi, 1991; Ogbu, 1987; Waters, 1994, 1999).

This section illustrates how Korean American students' educational attainment and aspirations are fundamentally based on larger social forces: the socioeconomic backgrounds of their families; access to social capital at home, in their communities, and in school; and structural support and caring relationships with teachers and counselors at school (Lew, 2004). In order to understand *how* and *why* low-status Korean American high school dropouts are limited in accessing and accumulating resources embedded in social networks, researchers may benefit from critically examining variability within the co-ethnic communities in the form of social class, schooling resources, and network orientation. In the context of limited social, economic, and institutional resources, low-status Korean American high school dropouts operated under a different network orientation than their MH counterparts. That is, if social capital derives from social relationships, then different groups of students have varying degrees of advantage and investment based on class, race, and institutional resources within the network. Thus, social networks are also implicated in the reproduction of inequality (Bourdieu & Passeron, 1977; Lareau, 1987, 2003; Lin, 2000; Stanton-Salazar, 1997, 2001; Willis, 1977). The findings point to the significance of institutional context when accounting for the relative disadvantages and obstacles experienced by poor communities in building social capital toward economic advancement. By examining social capital using an institutional and process-oriented approach, one can identify organizational forms and key actors critical to social capital building—a process that is deeply divided along class and racial lines (Saegert et al., 2001).

In order to negotiate and resist such institutional barriers in their homes, schools, and communities, these low-income Korean American students dropped out of high school and adopted behaviors that were not conducive to school achievement (Gibson & Ogbu, 1991; Lew, 2003a, 2004, in press; Matute-Bianchi, 1986, 1991; Ogbu, 1987). That said, these findings also complicate earlier understandings of oppositional cultural frames of reference and "acting White": In the context of a binary Black-and-White racial discourse, as well as the prevalent model minority stereotype that conflates Asian Americans with Whiteness, working-class Korean American high school dropouts' experiences were profoundly revealing. While the students internalized the model minority stereotype by connecting "successful" Asians and Koreans to Whiteness, they also resisted such a stereotype for themselves. By distinguishing themselves from wealthy and educated Koreans and Asians who symbolically represented Whiteness, they identified themselves with other "minorities"—a collective term symbolizing downward mobility and struggles with racism and poverty. When addressing issues of Asian American children and education, race and class continue to matter: As the findings of this research illustrate, it is important to distinguish the variability of social class and network orientation, highlight the fluidity of multiple identities, and examine institutional factors and schooling resources among Asian American children.

CHAPTER 6

Conclusion: Lessons from Korean American Communities

When accounting for Asian American academic achievement, class, race, and schooling contexts do matter. Unfortunately, these structural factors are rarely examined in educational research. Instead, a cultural discourse positing Asian Americans as a homogeneous model minority continues to prevail: The values of education, the work ethic, and the nuclear family continue to be the most common explanations for Asian American children's educational achievement. That is, Asian American achievement has been basically understood to be a result of this group's purportedly inherent cultural values and characteristics.

It is important to remember, however, that the model minority construct was not created by Asian Americans themselves but was thrust upon them in the form of this dominant cultural discourse. While presumed as positive, the dominant "success story" image conceals disparities among Asian American children in their educational achievement and socioeconomic backgrounds, and it obscures important structural barriers faced by many poor, minority children. The model minority stereotype mythologizes the economic and social success of Asian Americans; legitimates institutional racism and poverty; sustains hope of the American Dream; displaces society's failure regarding other disadvantaged minorities; and negates social, economic, and institutional barriers faced by underprivileged children. In the end, model minority discourse, as a hegemonic device, attributes academic success *and* failure to individual merit and cultural orientation, while underestimating important structural and institutional resources that all children need in order to achieve academically.

How we challenge the prevailing cultural discourse of individual meritocracy in education is of utmost importance, particularly as schools are faced with increasing racial segregation, high school dropouts, and standardized exams. As this research shows, how Asian American students learn to convert their aspirations and acceptance of the value of education into concrete schooling support toward academic achievement has more to do with an important set of structural resources that all students need—academic support and school guidance, access to key institutional gatekeepers in and outside of schools, and the family's economic and social resources. To underestimate these structural resources for Asian Americans in the name of model minority status would mean ignoring important social and economic contexts within which to frame *all* students' academic achievement. To that end, this research may have some important implications for future education policy and research. I turn to this discussion next.

IMPLICATIONS FOR EDUCATION POLICY

Parental Involvement

As illustrated in this research, the strategies adopted by Korean American parents depended on their socioeconomic backgrounds, as well as access to bilingual and educational resources. These patterns of parental strategies illustrate how variability of class and network orientation affects the ways in which two groups of parents provide educational support for their children and, ultimately, help their children bridge the gap between their schooling aspirations and achievement.

It is also worth noting, however, that despite these varying strategies employed by Korean immigrant parents, they are both at a disadvantage compared to middle-class White parents who are fluent in English and work in the mainstream economy. Both groups of Korean immigrant parents are limited in English-language skills and knowledge of the U.S. school system—factors that greatly inhibited their ability to help their children daily with schooling or with college preparation and counseling. To compensate for their limitations, the middle-class Korean parents—with their educational backgrounds, socioeconomic resources, and social capital—resorted to hiring private tutors and counselors and to enrolling their children in after-school academies in ethnic enclaves, which provide additional educational support for their children. As mentioned, these private after-school options provide direct schooling support and college guidance that Korean immigrant parents otherwise may not be able to give directly to their children. To achieve this end, the Korean immigrant parents in this research spend their personal funds on these private, tuition-based schools—which means they need to possess adequate economic and social resources in the first place. The Korean dropouts, who are poor and often come from single-parent households, on the other hand, cannot readily afford such private tuition and are more likely to work after school in order to compensate for their limited family income. They are also more likely to navigate schooling alone, without much adult guidance at home or in their communities and schools.

Given that increasing number of Asian American parents in today's schools are first-generation immigrants with limited English proficiency and knowledge of the U.S. education system, it is imperative that schools reach out to parents and provide appropriate resources. As illustrated in this study, bilingual support is especially important for poor immigrant parents who may have limited access to such resources in their co-ethnic communities. It is pivotal for schools to provide adequate bilingual assistance and translated materials so that immigrant parents are equipped with resources that enable them to be actively involved in schools. Moreover, Asian immigrant parents need to be educated on their legal rights regarding bilingual assistance and the tendency their children face of being "pushed" out of school systems; such education is crucial if they are to advocate for and make truly informed decisions on behalf of their children—and be full participants in their children's schools. The findings in this research challenge the popular sentiment that Asian and other immigrant parents are more likely to be passive and uninvolved in their children's schools, citing these and the aforementioned structural barriers as the real culprits.

This has been corroborated by other studies as well. For instance, in their research on immigrant parents and children, Ruiz-de-Valasco and Fix (2000) found that there were stark differences in how LEP/immigrant parents and teachers viewed the parents' involvement in their children's schooling. "Educators tend to rely on parents to be informed about their children's progress, act as advocates for their children, and frame student planning and goal setting" (p. 62). But instead, teachers often described immigrant parents, again, as being passive and uninvolved, pointing to their lack of school involvement and attributing this to their limited time and resources. However, when Ruiz-de-Valasco and Fix (2000) asked immigrant parents about the key factors that discouraged their participation in schools, parents told a different story. Although time and economic constraints were factors, most parents cited language barriers as the main obstacle to school participation. "Many parents noted that their children's English language ability was stronger than their own, and that they did not feel competent speaking with monolingual teachers or administrators about their children's schooling. As a result, they depended on their children to interpret for them and help them understand school norms and expectations" (p. 63). Conversely, the most important reason cited for immigrant parental involvement was bilingual outreach efforts by school staff and encouragement from other parents who spoke their native language.

Community-Based Organizations

In addition to schools, nonprofit and community-based organizations can also provide important resources for the growing number of immigrant parents and their children. Nonprofit community organizations play a pivotal role in Asian immigrant communities. Some of these groups provide human service programs and legal aid to the most disenfranchised Asian communities per their mission and specialization, as proven with the Korean high school dropouts in this study. These organizations are equipped with important bilingual assistance and in-depth cultural and historical knowledge of the communities they serve.

At the same time, these nonprofit organizations are, for the most part, poorly funded and find it difficult to collaborate effectively with large public institutions such as the New York public school system. However, by working together with local community organizations, the public school system would benefit greatly from their expertise, including their bilingual assistance and in-depth knowledge of the various Asian American communities they serve. This kind of effective collaboration is all the more important because of the growing number and diversity of Asian American children, which is posing an ever greater challenge to New York City schools to provide them with adequate academic support. Likewise, the community-based organizations would also benefit from working with the school systems, where they can learn how best to work with teachers, counselors, and administrators in assisting Asian American children and their parents. Moreover, by being involved with the school system, the community-based organizations can have a direct impact on policy development and implementation of school reform efforts.

School Context

As we critically examine how parents and communities influence student achievement, it is important not to lose sight of the significant role of schools themselves. This research illustrates how Asian American children's ability to translate educational aspirations into academic achievement depends not only on economic and social support from their parents and communities but also on the institutional characteristics of the school—how it provides schooling resources, reinforces accumulation of social capital, and fosters trusting and caring relations between students and teachers. However, classrooms and schools, for the most part, are structurally organized to enhance the type of socialization most associated with the transmission of privileged knowledge and the development of White middle-class ideologies (Bowles & Gintis, 1976). This has implications for the Korean American students in the study, given that, generally speaking, working-class minority and immigrant children come to schools with different cultural resources. Consequently, while they may be competent decoders in any number of cultural domains within their communities, they usually face barriers within mainstream institutions, such as schools and the workforce. In order for these children to learn decoding skills for crossing disparate sociocultural borders—say, between home and school—they need integral ties to institutional agents and gatekeepers in their school and community who can provide access to important schooling support. In short, children of Asian and other immigrants need access to institutional agents both *in and outside* of their co-ethnic networks for them to achieve in schools.

In addition, Asian American students are also a diverse lot who actively adapt to, negotiate, and resist the given structures around them. Consequently, the second-generation Korean children learn to reconstruct their own peer networks in order to gain many of the aforementioned resources, including emotional support for issues specific to them as children of immigrants: schooling and college guidance, job opportunities, intergenerational conflicts, and racial and ethnic identity issues. Through their own second-generation youth networks, both groups of Korean American students acquired resources that they could not readily get at home. However, given the different resources embedded in their respective schools and networks, the Korean students at MH were more likely than the Korean high school dropouts to access key gatekeepers in and outside of schools to help them achieve academically. In other words, while the Korean students at MH mostly used their networks to *advance* their academic and socioeconomic status, the Korean high school dropouts mostly used their networks to *overcome* academic and socioeconomic barriers.

SALIENCE OF RACE, ETHNICITY, AND CLASS

Meanwhile, if schools and class matter for Asian American students, so does race. Asian American students often face racial harassment and violence in and outside of urban schools. As noted in this research, both groups of Korean students faced racial harassment, but the Korean high school dropouts were more likely to face violence and fear within their school contexts. Too often, Asian American children are forced to navigate such racial harassment without adequate support and intervention by teachers or counselors. We can attribute this trend, in part, to the model minority discourse that paints Asian American students as invisible entities who have few, if any, problems in schools. We can also attribute it to schools failing to see how class and race frame Asian American students' experiences.

These findings can lend important insight, especially in the midst of the emerging debate on post-1965 immigrants' adaptation to and racial incorporation into the United States. For instance, both the middle- and working-class Korean American students in this study were keenly aware of their racial minority status and the resulting barriers they faced. Consequently, they interpreted "becoming American" with Whiteness. But interestingly, the students were also careful to point out the integral intersection of race and *class* when referring to the term *American*, being careful to point out that becoming American also meant achieving economically on a par with middle-class White Americans. Not surprisingly, then, the ways in which the students negotiate becoming "American" has much to do with how they interpret racial barriers within their given opportunity structure. For the middle-class Korean students at MH, who were equipped with strong social capital at home, in their community, and in school, resisting racial barriers by using education as a strategy to achieve economic mobility was a plausible option. Meantime, the working-class Korean high school dropouts who had limited social capital at home, in their communities, and at school were more vulnerable to stratifying forces and learned to adopt an oppositional cultural frame of reference not conducive to schooling. Furthermore, they distinguished themselves not only from Whiteness but also from wealthy and studious Korean and other Asian Americans, signaling negative and exclusionary forces of class and social status inherent in co-ethnic networks.

Although a majority of the Korean students in this study lived in Queens, the dropouts were more likely to live in neighborhoods and attend schools that were economically and racially isolated. In their study, Orfield and colleagues (2004) corroborated this finding by showing that concentrated racial and economic isolation is an important predictor of dropout rates. Their data are supported by a Johns Hopkins University study on urban high schools, which found that among those where 90% or more of the students were of color, only 42% of all freshmen advanced to grade 12 (as cited in Orfield et al., 2004). This is not surprising, given that almost 9 out of 10 intensely segregated minority schools also suffer the effects of concentrated poverty, beset by less qualified and experienced teachers, remedial courses rather than a college-preparatory curriculum, and rampant school violence. Meanwhile, comparatively few Whites, including those who are poor, experience such problems in schools (Orfield et al., 2004).

Yet despite their location in poor, isolated, minority communities, positioned as they are to underserve the most needy of students, these inadequate schools are held to the same performance standards as better-equipped schools in a nation that places undue emphasis on standardized testing. Meanwhile, in the name of high expectations, much of the rhetoric around achievement ignores and glosses over the important disparities of class and race—and institutional resources—acutely affecting urban schools. As this research illustrates, this trend has several consequences, foremost among them being the increased likelihood that teachers and counselors will push out "problem" children to boost their respective high school's success rate, rather than help the neediest of cases by providing them with the resources they require to graduate. As educators and policy makers, we need to question how these standardized exams are measuring accountability and whether they are adequate indicators of school "success." We must also address how they are contributing to the likelihood of students dropping out, as students and educators alike fail to receive the proper institutional support to meet these expectations.

FUTURE RESEARCH

In the context of the rising number of post-1965 immigrants and their children as well as their settlement in concentrated metropolitan areas, our urban schools are faced with a new set of challenges. Education policy and research should take into account the needs of our changing urban schools and the students attending them, who are increasingly poor minorities, children of recent immigrant parents, and residentially and linguistically isolated.

As far as Asian American children and families are concerned, there are still glaring gaps in the research. During the last few decades, changing immigration patterns and demographics have been reshaping Asian American populations and the school systems that serve them. There is increasing variability of ethnicity, class, generation, professional background, and immigrant history among Asian American communities, which greatly affects their children's academic achievement and social mobility. Moreover, the role of gender, and its intersection with class and race, has not been adequately addressed and warrants further examination. Despite these trends, the issue of diversity across racial groups and within Asian American populations has been largely ignored.

As Slaughter-Defoe, Nakagawa, Takanishi, and Johnson (1990) have argued, societal stereotypes have historically influenced research design and theory development in the field of education. For instance, they argue that education research has typically examined schooling failure for Blacks, while predicting schooling success for Asians. The cultural deficits of African American children and families were often compared to the cultural merit of Asian American children and families. In doing so, education research has typically reinforced the stereotype of Blacks and Asians, while, over the years, the underlying cultural assumptions regarding African Americans and Asian Americans have changed little. It is important that researchers continue to challenge the stereotypes attached to various ethnic and racial groups by critically examining variability of school achievement across, as well as within, such groups. I would also add that it is important to draw relationships between racial and ethnic groups, taking note of both converging and diverging social and cultural factors.

To that end, it is pivotal to disaggregate achievement data by race and class as well as to accurately calculate graduation and dropout rates. Orfield and colleagues (2004) argued that the current dropout statistics—mostly based on the Center for Educational Statistics and the Current Population Survey—do not provide a clear picture of who is actually dropping out. Because states rarely disaggregate graduation rates by race or socioeconomic status, the extremely low graduation rates for racial and ethnic minorities, students with learning disabilities, low-income students, and students with limited English proficiency are actually "masked" and rarely given the special attention they need. Consequently, official dropout statistics can underestimate the magnitude of the problems associated with increasing racial and class stratification across the nation. According to Orfield and colleagues (2004), the United States expends "considerably more funds gathering and checking test data than we commit to accurately assessing whether students graduate from high school." They add that without sound policy implementation to generate such accurate data, "no state can say with precision what percentage of students actually earn a bona fide diploma. Moreover, the graduation and dropout estimates that most states have been accustomed to reporting were often grossly inaccurate and therefore misleading" (p. 7).

In addition to improving upon the aggregate data now relied on to gauge student achievement and dropout rates, researchers need to complement these large-scale quantitative studies with in-depth, small-scale qualitative studies so that educators can better understand the complex processes by which students and families in changing contexts negotiate and gain educational opportunities available to them. By implementing better quantitative and qualitative research methods, we can identity the structural and institutional processes that may inhibit and promote achievement for various groups of students. Through this combined method, educators can gain insight into the important relationships among race, class, gender, and the complex ways in which students negotiate and resist their given opportunity structure. We know that race, class, and gender matter. But additional qualitative studies can reveal how they might be important and demonstrate how these factors remain salient and fluid across different contexts. Addressing these important issues has the potential to positively impact the way schools educate our children.

Lastly, in order to critically examine as well as develop policy recommendations for how family, community, and school impact Asian American children, we have to situate these factors in the larger economic, social, and historical context. On the one hand, the post-1965 Asian immigrants reap the benefits of the civil rights movement and stand to gain opportunities unavailable to earlier Asian Americans and many other marginalized groups. On the other hand, they are also entering the United States at a time of declining industrial economy with growing global and technical skill requirements, a growing service-sector economy that is also accompanied by the gradual disappearance of middle-level job opportunities, and increasing racial and economic segregation of schools and neighborhoods. How the post-1965 immigrants and their children negotiate and resist these forces to carve out their American Dream is an important question to ask and warrants a close examination by researchers and educators as we move forward to provide equal educational opportunities for all children.

References

Abelmann, N., & Lie, J. (1995). *Blue dreams: Korean Americans and the Los Angeles riots.* Cambridge, MA: Harvard University Press.

Alba, R. (1990). *Ethnic identity: The transformation of White America.* New Haven, CT: Yale University Press.

Amato, P. R. (1987). Family processes in one-parent, stepparent, and intact families: The child's point of view. *Journal of Marriage and the Family, 49*(2), 327–337.

Anyon, J. (1997). *Ghetto schooling: A political economy of urban educational reform.* New York: Teachers College Press.

Asian American Federation of New York. (2001). *New census estimates tell two stories about Asian and Pacific Islander students.* New York: Asian American Federation of New York Census Information Center.

Asian American Federation of New York. (2002). *Census profile: New York City's Korean American population.* New York: Asian American Federation of New York Census Information Center.

Asian American Federation of New York. (2003). *Census study shows severe poverty among New York City's Asian American children.* New York: Asian American Federation of New York Census Information Center

Astone, N. M., & McLanahan, S. S. (1991). Family structure, parental practices and high school completion. *American Sociological Review, 56*(3), 309–320.

Astone, N. M., & McLanahan, S. S. (1994). Family structure, residential mobility, and school dropout: A research note. *Demography, 31*(4), 575–584.

Barringer, H. R., Gardner, R. W., & Levin, M. (1993). *Asians and Pacific Islanders in the United States.* New York: Russell Sage Foundation.

Bernstein, B. (1975). *Class, codes, and control.* London: Routledge & Kegan Paul.

Bourdieu, P. (1977). *Outline of a theory of practice.* Cambridge, England: Cambridge University Press.

Bourdieu, P., & Passeron, J. C. (1977). *Reproduction in education, society, and culture.* London: Sage.

Bowles, S., & Gintis, H. (1976). *Schooling in capitalist America.* New York: Basic Books.

Boykin, A. W. (1986). The triple quandary and the schooling of Afro-American children. In U. Neisser (Ed.), *School achievement of minority children: New perspectives* (pp. 57–92). London: Erlbaum.

Boykin, A. W., & Toms, F. (1985). Black child socialization: A conceptual framework. In J. McAdoo & J. McAdoo (Eds.), *Black children* (pp. 33–51). Beverly Hills, CA: Sage.

Bowdith, C. (1993). Getting rid of troublemakers: High school disciplinary procedures and the production of dropouts. *Social Problems*, *40*(4), 493–509.

Butterfield, S. A. (2004). "We're just Black": The racial and ethnic identities of second-generation West Indians in New York. In P. Kasinitz, J. H. Mollenkopf, & M. C. Waters (Eds.), *Becoming New Yorkers: Ethnographies of the new second generation* (pp. 288–312). New York: Russell Sage Foundation.

Caplan, N., Choy, M. H., & Whitmore, J. K. (1991). *Children of the boat people: A study of educational success*. Ann Arbor: University of Michigan Press.

Castle, G. P., & Kushner, G. (Eds.). (1981). *Persistent peoples: Cultural enclaves in perspective*. Tucson: University of Arizona Press.

Chan, S. (1991). *Asian Americans: An interpretive history*. New York: Twayne.

Chaplin, D. (1999). *GEDs for teenagers: Are there unintended consequences?* Washington, DC: Urban Institute.

Coleman, J. S., & Hoffer, T. (1987). *Public and private high schools*. New York: Basic Books.

Croninger, R. G., & Lee, V. E. (2001). Social capital and dropping out of high school: Benefits to at-risk students of teachers' support and guidance. *Teachers College Press*, *104*(4), 548–581.

De Graaf, N. D., & Flap, H. D. (1988). "With a little help from my friends": Social resources as an explanation of occupational status and income in West Germany, the Netherlands, and the United States. *Social Forces*, *67*, 453–472.

Delpit, L. D. (1988). The silenced dialogue: Power and pedagogy in educating other people's children. *Harvard Educational Review*, *58*, 280–298.

De Vos, G. A. (Ed.). (1973). *Socialization for achievement: Essays on the cultural psychology of the Japanese*. Berkeley: University of California Press.

De Vos, G. A. (1980). Ethnic adaptation and minority status. *Journal of Cross-Cultural Psychology*, *11*(1), 101–124.

Division of Assessment and Accountability. (2000). *NYC public schools: 1998–99 annual school report*. New York: Author.

Division of Assessment and Accountability. (2002). *NYC public schools: 2000–01 annual school report*. New York: Author.

Dornbusch, S. M., Carlsmith, J. M., Bushwall, S. J., Ritter, P. L., Leiderman, H., Hastorf, A. H., & Gross, R. T. (1985). Single parents, extended households, and the control of adolescents. *Child Development*, *56*(2), 326–341.

Duncan, G. J., & Hoffman, S. D. (1985). A reconsideration of the economic consequences of marital dissolution. *Demography*, *22*(4), 485–497.

Ekstrom, R. B., Goertz, M. E., Pollack, J. M., & Rock, D. A. (1986). Who drops out of high school and why? Findings from a national study. *Teachers College Record*, *87*(3), 356–373.

Espiritu, Y. L. (1994). The intersection of race, ethnicity, and class: The multiple identities of second-generation Filipinos. *Identities*, *9*(1), 249–273.

Fine, M. (1991). *Framing drop-outs: Notes on the politics of an urban public high school*. Albany: State University of New York Press.

Foner, N. (1985). Race and color: Jamaican migrants in London and New York City. *International Migration Review*, *13*(2), 284–313.

Fong, T. P., & Shinagawa, L. H. (Eds.). (2000). *Asian Americans: Experiences and perspectives*. Englewood Cliffs, NJ: Prentice Hall.

Fordham, S., & Ogbu, J. U. (1986). Black student's school success: Coping with the "burden of 'acting white'." *The Urban Review*, *18*, 176–204.

Furstenberg, F, Jr., Gunn, J. B., & Morgan, P. (1987). *Adolescent mothers in later life*. New York: Cambridge University Press.

Gans, H. J. (1979). Symbolic ethnicity: The future of ethnic groups and cultures in America. *Ethnic and Racial Studies*, *2*(1), 1–20.

Gans, H. J. (1992). Second generation decline: Scenarios for the economic and ethnic futures of the post-1965 American immigrants. *Ethnic and Racial Studies*, *15*(2), 173–192.

Gee, J. P. (1989). Literacy, discourse, and linguistics: Introduction. *Journal of Education*, *171*(1), 5–17.

Gibson, M. A. (1988). *Accommodation without assimilation*. Ithaca, NY: Cornell University.

Gibson, M. A., & Ogbu, J. U. (Eds.). (1991). *Minority status and schooling: A comparative study of immigrant and involuntary minorities*. New York: Garland.

Glazer, N., & Moynihan, D. P. (1963). *Beyond the melting pot: The Negroes, Puerto Ricans, Jews, Italians and Irish of New York City*. Cambridge, MA: MIT Press and Harvard University Press.

Gottlieb, B. (1991). Social support in adolescence. In M. E. Colten & S. Gore (Eds.), *Adolescent stress: Causes and consequences* (pp. 281–306). New York: De Gruyter.

Granovetter, M. S. (1985). Economic action and social structure: The problem of embeddedness. *American Journal of Sociology*, *91*(3), 481–510.

Hallinan, M. T., & Sorensen, A. B. (1985). Ability grouping and student friendships. *American Educational Research Journal*, *22*(4), 485–499.

Hallinan, M. T., & Williams, R. A. (1990). Students' characteristics and the peer-influence process. *Sociology of Education 63*(2), 122–132.

Hing, B. O. (1993). *Making and remaking Asian American through immigration policy: 1850–1990*. Stanford, CA: Stanford University Press.

Hirschman, C., Kasinitz, P., & DeWind, J. (Eds.). (1999). *The handbook of international migration*. New York: Russell Sage Foundation.

Hirschman, C., & Wong, M. G. (1986). The extraordinary educational attainment of Asian Americans: A search for historical evidence and explanations. *Social Forces*, *65*(1), 1–27.

Holland, J. V., Kaplan, D. M., & Davis, S. D. (1974). Interschool transfers: A mental health challenge. *Journal of School Health*, *44*, 74–79.

Hsia, J. (1988). *Asian Americans in higher education and at work*. Hillsdale, NJ: Erlbaum.

Hsu, F. L. K. (1971). *The challenge of the American Dream: The Chinese in the United States*. Belmont, CA: Wadsworth.

Hune, S., & Chan, K. S. (2000). Educating Asian Pacific Americans: Struggles and progress. In T. P. Fong & L. H. Shinagawa (Eds.), *Asian Americans: Experiences and perspectives* (pp. 141–168). Englewood Cliffs, NJ: Prentice Hall.

Hurh, W. H., & Kim, K. C. (1984). *Korean immigrants in America: A structural analysis of ethnic confinement and adhesive adaptation*. Madison, NJ: Fairleigh Dickinson University Press.

Hurh, W. H., & Kim, K. C. (1989). The "success" image of Asian Americans: Its validity, and its practical and theoretical implications. *Ethnic and Racial Studies, 12*(4), 512–538.

Kao, G. (1995). Asian Americans as model minorities? A look at their academic performance. *American Journal of Education, 103*(2), 121–159.

Kao, G., & Tienda, M. (1998). Educational aspirations of minority youth. *American Journal of Education, 106*, 349–384.

Kasinitz, P., Mollenkopf, J. H., Waters, M. C. (Eds.). (2004). *Becoming New Yorkers: Ethnographies of the new second generation*. New York: Russell Sage Foundation.

Kasinitz, P., Mollenkopf, J., Waters, M., Lopez, N., & Kim, D. Y. (1997, October). *The school to work transition of second generation immigrants in metropolitan New York: Some preliminary findings*. Paper presented at the meeting of Levy Institute Conference on the Second Generation, Bard College, Annandale-on-Hudson, NY.

Kiang, P., & Kaplan, J. (1994). Where do we stand? Views on racial conflict by Vietnamese American high school students in a Black-and-White context. *Urban Review, 26*(2), 95–119.

Kibria, N. (2002). *Becoming Asian American: Second-generation Chinese and Korean American identities*. Baltimore, MD: Johns Hopkins University Press.

Kim, C. J. (2000). *Bitter fruit: The politics of the Black–Korean conflict in New York City*. New Haven, CT: Yale University Press.

Kim, D. Y. (2004). Leaving the ethnic economy: The rapid integration of second-generation Korean Americans in New York. In P. Kasinitz, J. H. Mollenkopf, & M. C. Waters (Eds.), *Becoming New Yorkers: Ethnographies of the new second generation* (pp. 154–196). New York: Russell Sage Foundation.

Kim, E. H. (1993). Home is where the han is: A Korean American perspective in Los Angeles riots. In R. Goodling-Williams (Ed.), *Reading Rodney King/Reading urban uprising* (pp. 215–235). New York: Routledge.

Kim, E. H., & Yu, E. (1996). *East to America: Korean American life stories*. New York: New Press.

Kim, E. Y. (1993). Career choice among second-generation Korean Americans: Reflections of a cultural model of success. *Anthropology and Education Quarterly, 24*(3), 224–248.

Kim, H. (Ed.). (1977). *The Korean diaspora: Historical and sociological studies of Korean immigration and assimilation in North America*. Santa Barbara, CA: ABC-Clio.

Kim, I. (1981). *New urban immigrants: The Korean community in New York*. Princeton, NJ: Princeton University Press.

Kim, K. C. (Ed.). (1999). *Koreans in the hood: Conflict with African Americans*. Baltimore, MD: Johns Hopkins University Press.

Krein, S. F., & Beller, A. H. (1988). Educational attainment of children from single-parent families: Differences by exposure, gender, and race. *Demography, 25*(2), 221–234.

Kwon, H. Y., Kim, K. C., & Warner, R. S. (2001). *Korean Americans and their religions: Pilgrims and missionaries from a different shore*. University Park: Pennsylvania State University Press.

Kwong, P. (1996). *The new Chinatown*. New York, NY: HarperCollins.

Lareau, A. (1987). Social class differences in family–school relationships: The importance of cultural capital. *Sociology of Education, 60*, 73–85.

Lareau, A. (2003). *Unequal children: Class, race, and family life*. Berkeley: University of California Press.

Lee, S. (2004). Class matters: Racial and ethnic identities of working- and middle-class second-generation Korean Americans in New York City. In P. Kasinitz, J. H. Mollenkopf, & M. C. Waters (Eds.), *Becoming New Yorkers: Ethnographies of the new second generation* (pp. 154–196). New York: Russell Sage Foundation.

Lee, S. J. (1996). *Unraveling the "model minority" stereotype: Listening to Asian American youth*. New York: Teachers College Press.

Lee, V. E., & Burkham, D. T. (1992). Transferring high schools: An alternative to dropping out? *American Journal of Education, 100*(4), 420–453.

Lew, J. (2003a). Korean American high school dropouts: A case study of their experiences and negotiations of schooling, family, and communities. In S. Books (Ed.), *Invisible children in the society and its schools* (pp. 53–66). Mahwah, NJ: Erlbaum.

Lew, J. (2003b). (Re)Construction of second-generation ethnic networks: Structuring academic success of Korean American high school students. In C. C. Park, S. J. Lee, & A. L. Goodwin (Eds.), *Research on the education of Asian Pacific Americans* (Vol. II) (pp. 157–176). Greenwich, CT: Information Age Publishing.

Lew, J. (2004). The "other" story of model minorities: Korean American high school dropouts in an urban context. *Anthropology Education Quarterly, 35*(3), 297–311.

Lew, J. (in press). A structural analysis of success and failure among Asian Americans: A case of Korean Americans in urban schools. *Teachers College Record.*

Light, I., & Bonacich, E. (1988). *Immigrant entrepreneurs: Koreans in Los Angeles 1965–1982*. Berkeley: University of California Press.

Light, I., & Gold, S. J. (2000). *Ethnic economies*. San Diego: Academic Press.

Lin, N. (1990). Social resources and social mobility: A structural theory of status attainment. In R. Breiger (Ed.), *Social mobility and social structure* (pp. 247–271). Cambridge, England: Cambridge University Press.

Lin, N. (2000). *Social capital: A theory of social structure and action*. Cambridge, England: Cambridge University Press.

Louie, V. S. (2001). Parents' aspirations and investment: The role of social class in the educational experiences of 1.5- and second-generation Chinese Americans. *Harvard Educational Review, 71*(3), 438–474.

Louie, V. S. (2004). *Compelled to excel: Immigration, education, and opportunity among Chinese Americans*. Stanford, CA: Stanford Press.

Lowe, L. (1996). *Immigrant acts*. Durham, NC: Duke University Press.

Mark, D. M. L., & Chih, G. (1982). *A place called America*. Dubuque, IA: Kendall Hunt.

Massey, D. S., & Denton, N. A. (1993). *American apartheid: Segregation and the making of the underclass*. Cambridge, MA: Harvard University Press.

Matute-Bianchi, M. E. (1986). Ethnic identities and patterns of school success and failure among Mexican-descent and Japanese-American students in a California high school: An ethnographic analysis. *American Journal of Education*, *95*(1), 233–255.

Matute-Bianchi, M. E. (1991). Situational ethnicity and patterns of school performance among immigrant and nonimmigrant Mexican-descent students. In M. A. Gibson & J. U. Ogbu (Eds.), *Minority status and schooling: A comparative study of immigrant and involuntary minorities* (pp. 205–247). New York: Garland.

MacLeod, J. (1995). *Ain't no makin' it: Aspirations and attainment in a low-income neighborhood*. Boulder, CO: Westview.

McLanahan, S. R. (1985). Family structure and the intergenerational transmission of poverty. *American Journal of Sociology*, *90*, 873–901.

McNeal, R. B., Jr. (1997). Are students being pulled out of high school? The effect of adolescent employment on dropping out. *Sociology of Education*, *70*(3), 206–220.

Min, P. G. (1995). *Asian Americans: Contemporary trends and issues*. Thousand Oaks, CA: Sage Publications.

Min, P. G. (1996). *Caught in the middle: Korean communities in New York*. Berkeley: University of California Press.

Min, P. G. (1998). *Changes and conflicts: Korean immigrant families in New York*. Needham Heights, MA: Allyn & Bacon.

Mordkowitz, E. R., & Ginsberg, H. P. (1987). Early academic socialization of successful Asian-American college students. *Quarterly Newsletter of the Laboratory of Comparative Human Cognition*, *9*, 85–91.

National Association of Korean American Service and Education Consortium. (1998). *A demographic profile of Korean Americans*. New York: Author.

Natriello, G. (Ed.). (1986). *School dropouts: Patterns and policies*. New York: Teachers College Press.

Natriello, G., McDill, E. L., & Pallas, A. M. (1990). *Schooling disadvantaged children: Racing against catastrophe*. New York: Teachers College Press.

Neisser, U. (Ed.). (1986). *The school achievement of minority children: New perspective*. Hillsdale, NJ: Erlbaum.

Newmann, F. M., Wehlage, G. G., & Lamborn, S. D. (1992). *Student engagement and achievement in American secondary schools*. New York: Teachers College Press.

New York City Board of Assessment. (2003). *Annual school report*. New York: New York City Board of Education.

Noddings, N. (1992). *The challenge to care in schools: An alternative approach to education*. New York: Teachers College Press.

Noguera, P. (2003). *City schools and the American Dream: Reclaiming the promise of public education*. New York: Teachers College Press.

Ogbu, J. U. (1987). Variability in minority school performance: A problem in search of an explanation. *Anthropology & Education Quarterly*, *18*(4), 312–334.

Okihiro, G. (1994). *Margins and mainstreams: Asians in American history and culture*. Seattle: University of Washington Press.

Omi, M., & Winant, H. (1986). *Racial formation in the United States: From the 1960s to the 1990s*. London: Routledge.

Orfield, G., & Eaton, S. (1996). *Dismantling desegregation.* New York: New Press.

Orfield, G., Losen, D., Wald, J., & Swanson, C. (2004). *Losing our future: How minority youths are being left behind by the graduation rate crisis.* Cambridge, MA: The Civil Rights Project at Harvard University. Contributors: Advocates for Children of New York, The Civil Society Institute.

Pang, V. O., & Cheng, L. L. (Eds.). (1998). *Struggling to be heard: The unmet needs of Asian Pacific American children.* Albany: State University of New York Press.

Park, C. C., Lee, S. J., & Goodwin, A. L. (Eds.). (2003). *Research on the education of Asian Pacific Americans* (Vol. II). Greenwich, CT: Information Age Publishing.

Park, K. (1997). *The Korean American Dream: Immigration and small business in New York City.* Ithaca, NY: Cornell University Press.

Phelan, P., Davidson, A. L., & Yu, H. C. (1993). Student's multiple worlds: Navigating the borders of family, peer, and school culture. In P. Phelan & A. L. Davidson (Eds.), *Renegotiating cultural diversity in American schools* (pp. 52–88). New York: Teachers College Press.

Pong, S. L., & Ju, D. B. (2000). The effects of change in family structure and income on dropping out of middle and high school. *Journal of Family Issues, 21*(2), 147–169.

Portes, A. (1988). Social capital: Its origins and applications in modern sociology. *Annual Review of Sociology, 24,* 1–24.

Portes, A., & Rumbaut, R. G. (1996). *Immigrant America: A portrait.* Berkeley: University of California Press.

Portes, A., & Rumbaut, R. G. (2001). *Legacies: The story of the immigrant second generation.* Berkeley: University of California Press.

Portes, A., & Zhou, M. (1993). The new second generation: Segmented assimilation and its variants. *Annals of the American Academy, 530,* 74–96.

Public education crisis: Parents question role of education ministry. (2003, November 20). *Korea Times.* Retrieved July 20, 2004, from http://times.hankooki.com

Ruiz-de-Valasco, J., & Fix, M. (2000). *Overlooked & underserved: Immigrant students in U.S. secondary schools.* Washington, DC: Urban Institute.

Rumbaut, R. G., & Cornelius, W. A. (Eds.). (1995). *California's immigrant children: Theory, research and implications for educational policy.* Center for U.S.–Mexican Studies: University of California, San Diego.

Rumberger, R. W., Ghatak, R., Poulos, G., Ritter, P. L., & Dornbusch, S. M. (1990). Family influence on dropout behavior in one California high school. *Sociology of Education, 63*(4), 283–299.

Rumberger, R. W., & Larson, K. A. (1998). Student mobility and the increased risk of high school dropout. *American Journal of Education, 107*(1), 1–35.

Saegert, S., Thompson, J. P., & Warren, M. (Eds.). (2001). *Social capital and poor communities.* New York: Russell Sage Foundation.

Sanders, J. M., & Nee, V. (1987). Limits of ethnic solidarity in the enclave economy. *American Sociological Review, 52*(61), 745–773.

Schneider, B., & Lee, Y. (1990). A model for academic success: The school and home environment of East Asian students. *Anthropology and Education Quarterly, 21,* 358–377.

Slaughter-Defoe, D. T., Nakagawa, K., Takanishi, R., & Johnson, D. (1990). Toward cultural/ecological perspective on schooling and achievement in African- and Asian-American children. *Child Development*, *61*(2), 363–383.

Spicer, E. H., & Thompson, R. H. (1972). *Plural society in the Southwest.* Albuquerque: University of New Mexico Press.

Stack, C. (1974). *All our kin: Strategies for survival in the Black community.* New York: Harper & Row.

Stanton-Salazar, R. D. (1997). A social capital framework. *Harvard Education Review*, *87*(1), 1–40.

Stanton-Salazar, R. D. (2001). *Manufacturing hope and despair: The school and kin support networks of U.S.–Mexican youth.* New York: Teachers College Press.

Stanton-Salazar, R. D., & Dornbusch, S. M. (1995). Social capital and the social reproduction of inequality: The formation of informational networks among Mexican-origin high school students. *Sociology of Education*, *68*, 116–135.

Stanton-Salazar, R. D., & Spina, S. U. (2005). Adolescent peer networks as a context for social and emotional support. *Youth & Society*, *36*, 379–417.

Suárez-Orozco, M. (2001). Globalization, immigration, and education: The research agenda. *Harvard Educational Review*, *71*(3), 345–365.

Suárez-Orozco, C., & Suárez-Orozco, M. (1995). *Transformations: Immigration, family, life, and achievement motivation among Latino adolescents.* Stanford, CA: Stanford University Press.

Suárez-Orozco, C., & Suárez-Orozco, M. (2001). *Children of immigration.* Cambridge, MA: Harvard University Press.

Sue, S., & Okazaki, S. (1990). Asian-American educational achievements: A phenomenon in search of an explanation. *American Psychologist*, *45*(8), 913–920.

Sui-Chu, E. H., & Willms, J. D. (1996). Effects of parental involvement on eighth-grade achievement. *Sociology of Education*, *69*(2), 126–141.

Sung, B. L. (1987). *The adjustment experience of Chinese immigrant children in New York City.* New York: Center for Migration Studies.

Suzuki, R. H. (1980). Education and the socialization of Asian Americans: A revisionist analysis of the "model minority" thesis. In R. Endo, S. Sue, & N. N. Wagner (Eds.), *Asian Americans: Social and psychological perspectives* (Vol. 2) (pp. 155–175). Ben Lomond, CA: Science and Behavior Books.

Takaki, R. (1989). *Strangers from a different shore.* New York: Penguin.

Tuan, M. (1998). *Forever foreigners or honorary Whites? The Asian ethnic experience today.* New Brunswick, NJ: Rutgers University Press.

Urban Institute (2000). *One in five U.S. children are children of immigrants: Checkpoints.* Washington, DC: Author.

U.S. Bureau of the Census. (1993). *1990 Census of population: The Asians and Pacific Islanders in the United States* (1990 CP-3-5). Washington, DC: U.S. Government Printing Office.

U.S. Bureau of the Census. (1999). *School enrollment in the United States—Social and economic characteristics of students.* Current Population Reports. Washington, DC: U.S. Government Printing Office.

U.S. Bureau of the Census. (2001). *Census 2000 Summary File 1* (SF1). Washington, DC: U.S. Government Printing Office.

U.S. Bureau of the Census. (2002). *Census 2000 Brief: The Asian population 2000.* Washington, DC: U.S. Government Printing Office.

Valenzuela, A. (1999). *Subtractive schooling: U.S.–Mexican youth and the politics of caring.* Albany: State University of New York Press.

Waters, M. C. (1990). *Ethnic options: Choosing identities in America.* Berkeley: University of California Press.

Waters, M. C. (1994). Ethnic and racial identities of second-generation Black immigrants in New York City. *International Migration Review, 28*(4), 795–820.

Waters, M. C. (1999). *Black identities: West Indian immigrant dreams and American realities.* Cambridge, MA: Harvard University Press.

Wehlage, G. G., & Rutter, R. A. (1986). Dropping out: How much do schools contribute to the problem? *Teachers College Record, 87*(3), 374–392.

Weinberg, M. (1997). *Asian-American education: Historical background and current realities.* Mahwah, NJ: Erlbaum.

Willis, P. E. (1977). *Learning to labour: How working class kids get working class jobs.* New York: Columbia University Press.

Woo, D. (2000). The inventing and reinventing of "model minorities": The cultural veil obscuring structural sources of inequality. In T. P. Fong & L. H. Shinagawa (Eds.), *Asian Americans: Experiences and perspectives* (pp. 193–212). Englewood Cliffs, NJ: Prentice Hall.

Zhou, M. (1997). Social capital in Chinatown: The role of community-based organizations and families in adaptation of the younger generation. In M. Seller & L. Weis (Eds.), *Beyond Black and White: New faces and voices in U.S. schools* (pp. 181–206). Albany: State University of New York Press.

Zhou, M., & Bankston, C. L., III. (1996). Social capital and the adaptation of the second generation: The case of Vietnamese youth in New Orleans. In A. Portes (Ed.), *The new second generation* (pp. 197–220). New York: Russell Sage Foundation.

Zhou, M., & Bankston, C. L., III. (1998). *Growing up American: How Vietnamese children adapt to life in the United States.* New York: Russell Sage Foundation.

Index

About the Author

Jamie Lew is an assistant professor in the Department of Urban Education at Rutgers University–Newark. Her research interests include race and ethnic relations, immigration and international migration, and urban schools and policy. Her current research examines the changing race and ethnic relations in urban and suburban schools in New York and New Jersey.